F. W. Maitland

G. R. Elton

F. W. Maitland

Yale University Press
New Haven and London

First published in the United Kingdom by
George Weidenfeld and Nicolson Ltd.
Published in the United States by Yale University Press.

Printed in Great Britain

Library of Congress catalogue card number: 85–40439
International standard book number: 0–300–03528–4

10 9 8 7 6 5 4 3 2 1

Contents

v

Preface

A long book could be written about F. W. Maitland, and short books have been. Even so, he is familiar only to fellow historians; the world at large knows too little about a man who possessed something very uncommon among even the best of his kind – a real touch of genius. That this book hopes to remedy this state of affairs goes without saying; whether it will do so is quite another question. A full review of Maitland's work would require far more room than I have at my disposal, and many of his achievements cannot in consequence be properly analysed. I shall try to get close to him at work – to see how he did it and what he made of it – by supplementing a general appraisal by a more careful look at four of his writings. Since Maitland was the kind of historian who all the time wrestles with specific and often highly technical problems of the past, I have found it necessary to follow him into those specific and technical discussions. Maitland without his land law, Maitland without his plea rolls, Maitland without his footnotes is not the real Maitland. He always remained comprehensible even to the uninitiated; I can only say that I have tried so far as I can to follow his example.

For the writing of this book I have one not uncommon qualification and two obvious disqualifications. The qualification consists of my unstinted admiration for Maitland; the disabilities arise from the fact that he was a historian of the law and of the middle ages, whereas I am neither. Admiration by itself produces only hagiography of which, in Maitland's case, we have had too much. But in order to submit such feelings to a fruitful discipline I have had to discuss him as though I had some standing in the history of the middle ages and the law. The folly of this pretence will doubtless be soon pointed out by the servitors of two exceptionally jealous gods, and no pleas of *peccavi* or in mitigation are likely to avail. None shall therefore be advanced. The book, which it took about four weeks to write but many years of study and reflection to make ready for, gave great pleasure to its author; *parva, ut spero, illius gaudii pars afficiat alios.*

A special part of that pleasure must, however, remain my own. To have been allowed to write about Maitland while being president of that Selden Society which owes its birth, survival and defined purpose almost entirely to him is an honour. Maitland never presided over the Society; he ran it as its literary director and most voluminous contributor. But times are not what they were. The literary directors, I am happy to say, still run it and contribute voluminously. But Maitland's first president was the Lord Chief Justice of England.

G. R. E.
September 1984

1 The Man

When Frederic William Maitland died, a large part of the world of learning went into mourning. The official journal of his own university, the *Cambridge University Reporter*, recorded his death in the customary brief note, but it also found itself compelled to enter a truly unique event. On 5 February 1907 there appeared in it an address of condolence from the University of Oxford, lamenting the death of 'one who has passed away in the full maturity of his powers; diligent beyond the limitations of feeble health; eager, strenuous and sympathetic; beloved by friends and disciples; respected and admired by the University of which he was so brilliant an ornament; and approved by the universal verdict of all serious students'.[1] This unprecedented tribute, which reads as though it had originally been composed in Latin but had been kindly translated for the better understanding of an institution of learning regarded as unlikely to comprehend a learned language, barely hid the conviction, ever since ingrained at Oxford, that Maitland had somehow come to labour in the wrong university. Most of his books were acquired by Oxford, to form the foundation of their History Faculty's library; after all, Cambridge surprisingly already possessed such a thing, created out of Sir John Seeley's bequest. As late as 1965 that quintessential Oxonian, Bruce McFarlane of Magdalen College, mocked Cambridge's alleged neglect of one of its greatest sons.[2] Certainly Maitland, who had many friends, lacked disciples in the Cambridge of his own day, though even then he had some in two continents and has ever since inspired a posthumous following in all sorts of places. Nor did Cambridge forget Maitland at once; not untypically, it settled down to debating how to preserve his memory. Some four months after entering the sister-university's tribute, the *Reporter*'s pages once more contained a unique entry – the full record of a long discussion (held not even on University premises but in Trinity College) concerning the memorial due to the great man.[3] Money had been collected which needed applying. There resulted, on the one hand, the F. W. Maitland Memorial Fund for the Study of the History of the Law (which has produced some valuable published lectures), and on the other a bronze bust placed in the University's Law Library. Maitland's comment on this outcome of committee thinking would be worth having. Maitland's own college, Downing, preserved both his study and his name in the title of a history society which continues to meet there and which will show the visiting lecturer the standing lectern on which Maitland did so much of his writing.

Other tributes also came in from the first. The *Law Quarterly Review*, an austere journal in which incomprehensible problems so regularly receive incomprehensible solutions, allotted fourteen pages to letters from eight foreign eminences.[4] Oliver Wendell Holmes, speaking for America, gave little sign that he had actually read any of Maitland's serious works but expressed admiration for the author of *The Life and Letters of Leslie Stephen*, the more or less filial chore which had kept the dying Maitland from his beloved Year Books. An old and regular correspondent, John C. Gray, wrote in suitable terms from Harvard. France sent two representatives, one of whom (Paul Meyer) signified the preoccupations of his nation by singling out Maitland's study of the old Law French. Even more typical were the two Germans. Heinrich Brunner, who was not entirely alone in regarding himself as the leading legal historian of his generation, praised with massive condescension. On the other hand, Felix Liebermann, a simple and unworldly character, transferred the crown for legal history to his English friend in a note full of true amiability which also, alas, included a typical German cliché when it called Maitland 'dieser geborene

Historiker' – this historian born, which, as it happened, was true only if Maitland was born at the age of about thirty. From Italy came A. Zocca-Rosa, and from Vienna Joseph Redlich, the one man in this galaxy who had been really close to Maitland and testified to their friendship in a touching threnody. With Redlich, Maitland, whose letters rarely unbuttoned, had used the bantering tone that had endeared him to those who lived with him. When Redlich offered to translate Maitland's complex essay on trust and corporation (a mixture of law, history and philosophy), Maitland, whose doubts had to be overcome as in the end they were, thanked him warmly. 'But,' he continued, 'you also frighten me. You German jurists are such terrible fellows that the more I think of addressing you the less I like it. I think I hear one saying "Nichts neues!" and another saying that all my notions of jurisprudence are addled and muddled.' It was also to Redlich that Maitland's widow wrote a truly affecting account of her husband's last days.[5] In that array of mourners at the wake, the courteous Austrian easily carried off the palm.

Since then, the chorus of praise has never ceased; in the eighty years that have passed since Maitland's death his name and fame have remained resplendent. The full tally would badly overload this account, but an indication must be given. In 1908, A. L. Smith, non-producing medievalist and eminent master of Balliol College, in opening the proposal for the Maitland Library, set the tone in some rather high-flown lectures.[6] Maitland, we are told, invented a 'new method' of analysis and synthesis; 'the salient quality of Maitland's style' was found in his concreteness; Maitland stood comparison with Macaulay (a very strange conceit); Maitland's relation to history was 'religious'. Two years later, Maitland's brother-in-law, Herbert Fisher, another historian who after a spell in politics became head of an Oxford college (New College, where I saw him a few days before his death in 1940), set the seal of close personal acquaintance on the image that was to prove lasting: 'The world lost in Maitland not only a great and original scholar but also a nature of singular charm and beauty.'[7] My citing this description, it should be emphasized, does not signify disagreement.

Many others rushed into print to commemorate a friend and a pattern of learning. A conscientious list, compiled in 1961, ran to forty-one items and a half-century of memories.[8] One of them merits a word. Some fifteen years after Maitland's death, William Buckland, Regius professor of civil law at Cambridge, used the initiation of a new journal to redress the balance somewhat by describing the human Maitland who, as he rather oddly put it, 'never pretended to undervalue those aspects of life which are not purely intellectual'. Maitland, we learn, had been an athlete in his youth; indeed, he was while his health lasted one of those formidable walkers that populated the Victorian intellectual scene. He became an enthusiastic though never very competent cyclist, an assessment supported by some of Maitland's own accounts of his cycling with failing brakes around the Canaries. Above all, he was a man of loyalty, one who would almost never change his mind about another person once he had made it up, though he could speak very critically, especially about established figures sitting on their eminence.[9] I find this last observation perhaps the most sympathetic thing I have seen said about Maitland.

And so he never died. His papers were collected by H. A. L. Fisher in 1911 and have since been twice reprinted selectively: mostly legal ones edited by H. Hazeltine and others in 1936, mostly historical ones edited by Helen Cam (with another enthusiastic preface) in 1957. Two historians of varied attainments have attempted to analyse Maitland the historian, less in an endeavour to discover what made him great than in a certain knowledge that he was great: H. E. Bell in an honest but uninspired piece of plod, and James R. Cameron in all the naive solemnity of an Oklahoma dissertation.[10] These are works of piety, despite occasional criticisms, that do not explain the phenomenon. More recently still we have had a brilliant and moving tribute from S. F. C. Milsom, who not only understands the phenomenon but stands alone in his ability to meet Maitland on his own ground; but a single lecture cannot exhaust the theme.[11] Most of Maitland's surviving letters are in print.[12] The ultimate mausoleum exists in what is effectively an official *Life*.[13] The personal recollections of his lively younger daughter are on record, as are those of Harry Hollond, professor of law at Cambridge, who when he died in 1974 removed from the scene the last man who had heard Maitland lecture.[14] As late as 1968, his University Press, in justified confidence that no money would be lost, brought out a paperback reprint of the famous *History of English Law*, a work known to generations simply as Pollock and Maitland. (Sir Frederick Pollock's contribution – a chapter on the Anglo-Saxons – is reliably reported to have caused Maitland to speed up his writing of the remainder, in order to prevent any more pieces coming from his collaborator.) Maitland remains on a pedestal, and the worshippers (all of them professional historians) continue to kneel around him – myself before this amongst them.[15] Even one self-confident non-scholar, unable, as he said, to understand Maitland's real work, chose to treat him as the pattern of excellence.[16] One can quite understand the touch of exasperation which led John Kenyon, a historian of the seventeenth century, to refer to this ever praised medievalist as 'the sainted Maitland'.[17]

Thus the claims of F. W. Maitland, so often asserted and so rarely dissected, do need investigation and explanation. Why should a historian who died three generations ago, whose working life extended to just over twenty years, who confined himself to the history of the middle ages and specialized in their law – why should he have been regarded by so many as beyond compare and so influential? How has he maintained his credit for so long, and what is it that his admirers admire? Above all, perhaps, stands the question whether they are right to admire him so. How great a historian was Maitland?

Maitland was born on 28 May 1850; his county, Gloucestershire, continued until 1898 to provide him with a holiday home in the modest family property called Horsepools. Both his father and his grandfather had had rather complicated careers in which a short and unsatisfactory engagement with the law had played a part. His grandfather, Samuel Roffey Maitland, in the end opted for the Church and the study of history; today he is chiefly remembered for the severe attack he mounted on John Foxe's *Book of Martyrs*, a scholarly and somewhat misleading contribution to the Tractarian Movement among Anglicans. His father, who at the end briefly served as secretary to the Civil Service Commission, lived the life of a rentier and never really fulfilled his potential. He died when Maitland was thirteen years old; with two sisters in the family, the boy grew up among women. School imbued him with a quirky but passionate distaste for the Greek language. He entered Trinity College, Cambridge, in October 1869 and pursued the typical career of a bright but aimless undergraduate, impressing his tutors by his intelligence and his fellows by his wit and his competence as a runner. Apparently he shone as an after-dinner speaker and a debater in the Apostles Club, once famous as the nursery of many talents though now more notorious as the nursery of the traitors of the 1930s. Such attainments can be judged only from reports, but Maitland always retained the gift of brilliant speech.

When he came to Cambridge, the only subjects to be studied for a degree were classics and mathematics. His abhorrence for Greek barred him from the first, but he did not shine at mathematics and never liked it. However, before he could lose his way completely he discovered what every bright undergraduate needs – a truly admired teacher. In his case the role was filled by the philosopher Henry Sidgwick, the most generous and least assertive of John Stuart Mill's disciples. Under Sidgwick's influence Maitland decided to switch to the study of philosophy, rendered possible by the very recent introduction of the Moral Sciences Tripos, and in 1872 he graduated with a first-class degree. He stayed on for a while to become president of the Union Society, where his debating skill and courtesy made his term of office memorable. Like father and grandfather he was uncertain about his future, but like father and grandfather he tried the law and moved to London. Called to the bar in 1876 he practised – that is to say, sat idle – for seven years in chambers in Lincoln's Inn. In 1875, an attempt to return to Cambridge failed when he was defeated in a fellowship competition at Trinity. This misfortune seemed to doom him to a professional career which did not in the least attract him. He managed to live a sober but amusing life in London, making the acquaintance of lifelong friends such as Leslie Stephen (1832–1904), about to become the grand old man of literary studies and founder of the *Dictionary of National Biography*, or Frederick Pollock (1845–1937), destined to become the longest-lived of eminent lawyers, or Paul Vinogradoff (1854–1925), a Russian scholar with a consuming interest in English medieval history and law who ended up in an Oxford chair. He joined the Tramps, a typically Victorian society (founded by Stephen and Pollock) which was dedicated to regular Sunday walks around the environs of London; the recorded intellectual activities associated with this group reek of a juvenile facetiousness which all of them should have outgrown long before.

The simple truth is that at this time Maitland had not so much lost his way as never discovered it. The law offered a boring way to fill the passing hours; it certainly offered to a rather diffident young man repelled by its absurdities no prospect of success or wealth. Maitland applied himself conscientiously and acquired an instinctive understanding of its spirit as well as a lasting conviction that the law of property in particular needed to be fundamentally reformed and relieved of the ridiculous and irrelevant medieval hangover. Philosophy had had its attraction, diminished though that was after his failure at Trinity; especially it enabled him to overcome the mindlessness of the common law, with its concentration on particulars. Maitland was always to display an inclination towards jurisprudence, an inclination which has never yet made for success at the bar. He found his salvation in 1884 when for the first time he visited the Public Record

Office. His own recollection that he did so under the direct inspiration of Vinogradoff seems to have been mistaken, but there is no doubt that what guided his steps were talks with Vinogradoff and perhaps others which revealed to him the wealth of information especially on the age of Bracton (the legal history of the thirteenth century) which lay but partially explored in that impressively absurd piece of Victorian Gothic in Chancery Lane. At any rate, he had at last discovered his vocation, though not one born so much as produced by his previous training and the accident that what took hold of his mind were the manuscript records, most of them produced by the processes of the law, of medieval England. That first sight of the parchment rolls, which he approached totally uninstructed even in the reading of the script and which he taught himself to decipher and understand, settled his future.

However, though now set on the road and resolved to be a historian, the face that the world thought it saw remained that of a lawyer. This happened beause in 1885 he returned to Cambridge in order to take up a readership in English law. He owed this blessing to Sidgwick who had personally endowed the readership in order to bring his most brilliant pupil back to the University. Then, in 1888, Maitland was elected Downing professor of the laws of England, and throughout his career he diligently lectured on such things as tort and real property, though also on constitutional history. His lectures on this last theme – very much the lectures of a constitutional lawyer – were published, contrary to his wishes, after his death; splendid lectures though they must have been to hear, they embodied a state of learning already out of date at the time of publication, and it was unfortunate that the book remained in undergraduate use for half a century. Too many people thus came to know the least characteristic side of Maitland through a screen of error mixed with inspiration. (One is best advised never to write one's lectures: then no one can ever publish them.) Maitland took a very active part in the professorial life of Cambridge, serving on the Library Syndicate, the much more interesting Press Syndicate, and the Council of the Senate. Speaking from experience, I can well understand his liking for the second and deeply admire his patience with the last, a body designed to teach men the mortification of the spirit. He examined regularly, and as regularly complained of it. He spoke in the Senate House on the academic issues of the day; a splendidly ironic speech on some halfhearted proposals of 1897 to admit women to the University's degree was long remembered. As so often at Cambridge, the cause of progress lost when it would have made sense for it to win; victory tends to come on occasions when there is little enough to be said for it. But Maitland had testified to both his wisdom and his wit, which could be savage, as on that occasion it justly was. These activities in University and College took their share of his time, and like all good scholars he lamented; had he known of the amount of time that was to be so preempted a century later he might have better appreciated his own fate.

His early years at Cambridge were marked by two significant events in which the University played no part. Late in 1886 a group of eminent lawyers met to found the Selden Society, dedicated to the publication of the historical materials of the law; whether the idea originated in Maitland's mind or not, he became in fact its chief lasting inspiration. As an untiring contributor of volumes and as the even more untiring promoter of other people's research – he remained the Society's literary director. to the end of his life – he set the course for a body whose publications have shaped the nature of English legal history. The work proved formidable, especially when in 1894 Edward Dove, the secretary and treasurer, shot himself just ahead of the discovery that he had embezzled all the funds. Maitland, who never ceased to speak of Dove in tones of sorrow rather than just fury, came to the rescue, mobilizing support and subventions. For the rest of his days the Society grew from strength to strength under the joint guidance of its literary director and its new secretary, Benjamin Lock – a cooperation between enthusiastic diligence and careful husbandry that brought instant success. Maitland's

9

many extant letters to Lock show him endlessly involved in planning volumes, seeking contributors, chivvying tardy men into unaccustomed activity, and reading proofs. Today the Selden Society stands as an enduring memorial to its effective founder, and I hope he would regard this as sufficient reward for all the hours he spent on its affairs.

The other event was Maitland's marriage, also in 1886, to Florence Fisher, sister-in-law to Leslie Stephen, at whose house Maitland met her. She was fourteen years younger than he, a sensible, generous, intelligent and (this mattered to Maitland) musically gifted product of the Victorian intellectual elite; she would also appear to have been the only person who called him Fred. If his mother or sisters did so, we do not know of it. The marriage, which produced two daughters improbably christened Fredigond and Ermengard (Maitland, a Wagnerian, did have the grace to be a trifle ashamed of this burden placed on his progeny), was a great success, and Maitland turned out to be an ideal husband and father. Unlike professoring and managing the Selden Society, his marriage assisted rather than hindered his scholarly work.

The mention of Maitland's first name permits a short detour into the epistolary manners of the later nineteenth century. They were, at least in Maitland's case but certainly not only in his, extraordinarily formal. One never used first names; only members of the family, and that included brother-in-law Herbert Fisher, were ever so addressed. At all other times Maitland used surnames, even to close friends of very long standing.[18] There was a well-graded progress from 'Dear Mr X' through 'Dear X' to 'My Dear X', the charting of which can reveal the history of an association. His wife he addressed as 'Beloved', signing himself 'F.'; to everybody else he was at the foot of the letter 'F. W. Maitland' – even to his sister and to Fisher – and mostly 'truly' or 'very truly'. The surface stiffness of these conventions hides some genuinely affectionate relationships. It may also be remarked that Maitland wrote two quite different hands. His usual script was upright, fast, fluent and very donnish, but on some occasions he used a manifestly slower and rounder hand, inclining to the right. Neither hand poses serious problems to the reader.[19] There seems to be neither rhyme nor reason in this; certainly the second hand is not a sign of advancing age or deteriorating health, nor does anything seem to depend on the solemnity or formality of the occasion. Surely Maitland must have known that he was presenting himself in this guise of a split or double personality: what was he up to?

Maitland's first published piece of historical writing resulted from that first visit to the P.R.O. when an idle interest in his county of birth had directed his search: the edition of pleas in Gloucestershire heard before a royal commissioner in 1221 (1884). The tyro effort forecast the master's hand. For the next twenty-two years Maitland's productivity never slackened; he worked extraordinarily fast while retaining accuracy and avoiding all superficiality . His rate of work would be miraculous in an age of photographic copying machines, word processors and research assistants; displayed by one who wrote every word by hand, took his notes from originals to be found only by travelling to London and often still poorly ordered, and did it all himself, it becomes transcendental. But the facts are there and need to be recited.[20]

In those twenty-two years Maitland published *The Pleas of the Crown for the County of Gloucester before the Abbot of Reading, 1221* (1884); *Justice and Police* (1885); with Frederick Pollock but really by himself, the two volumes of *The History of English Law before the Time of Edward I* (1895; second enlarged edition 1898); *Domesday Book and Beyond* (1897); *Township and Borough* (1898), which were his Ford lectures delivered at Oxford in 1897; *Roman Canon Law in the Church of England* (1898); *English Law and the Renaissance* (1901); *Trust and Corporation* (1904); *The Life and Letters of Leslie Stephen* (1906). After his death, two sets of lectures found among his papers were published: *The Constitutional History of England* (1907) and *Equity: also the Forms of Action at Common Law* (1909). By himself – and the occasional appearance of a co-editor on the title-page should not disguise who did nearly all the work – he edited a string of volumes which required, and got, in both text and introduction the sort of labours that go to the making of a book: three volumes of *Bracton's Note-Book* (1897); *Three Rolls of the King's Court, 1194–1195* (Pipe Roll Society, 1891); *Records of the Parliament Holden at Westminster, on the 28th Day of February, 1305* (Rolls Series, 1893); *Magistri Vacarii Summa de Matrimonio* (1898); with Mary Bateson, *The Charters of the Borough of Cambridge* (1901). For the Selden Society he produced *Select Pleas of the Crown* (1888), *Select Pleas in Manorial and other Seigniorial Courts* (1889), *The Court Baron* with W. P. Baildon (1891), *Select Passages from the Works of Bracton and Azo* (1895), and the first three volumes of the Society's Year Book series, covering the years 1307–11 (1903, 1905, 1907 posthumously). He did a large share of the collaborative work on the Eyre of Kent (three volumes, Selden Society, 1910, 1912, 1913) and in 1900 produced a translation of Otto Gierke's *Political Theories of the Middle Ages* with a long introduction which matched his text in learning and vastly surpassed it in elegance. He contributed important introductions to books edited by other hands, especially W. J. Whittaker's *The Mirror of Justices* (Selden Society, 1895) and L. Alston's *De Republica Anglorum by Sir Thomas Smith* (1906). He also wrote numerous articles and reviews, many of them very long; sixty-nine were reprinted in Fisher's collection (1911), which is not quite complete. Most of his work rested on hitherto unused or now and again misused source materials; he could hardly ever rely on previous work by other scholars.

This incessant labour went on against a background of deteriorating health. Maitland had never been a robust man, though wiry and tough enough in his younger days; the few surviving portraits (he did not like being photographed) show a man with never an ounce of flesh to spare. From the early 1890s onwards he became increasingly subject to attacks of ill-health, and by the end of the century he was a very sick man. Exactly what it was that he suffered from is not clear; one reads variously of tuberculosis and diabetes, but there appears to be no accurate record of symptoms. In his letters, he himself usually referred to the devil or the familiar fiend that seized him at intervals. The effects, however, were plain: increasingly he succumbed to total prostration and was forced to spend endless days in bed. The vile winter climate of Cambridge threatened to kill him, and from 1898 onwards he annually obeyed medical orders to seek the sun in October or November. Thereafter every winter was spent in the Canaries or on Madeira, a regime which involved complex journeys by sea with wife, daughters and baggage, the last for a while including his bicycle, which he rode around the steep mountains of the islands. The University very wisely tolerated the absences of the Downing professor, who, however, compensated for them by intensive lecture courses delivered when from March or thereabouts he returned to Cambridge. He did not cease to work but naturally found it increasingly difficult to adhere to his customary speed, nor could he in those conditions compose major works. Editing, especially of Year Books, could continue, and so he usually carried quantities of photostats to his winter exile. I shall, however, suggest another reason for his move from the writing of history to the production of the materials of historical research.[21]

Painful, debilitating and, to a man of his vigorous temperament, increasingly frustrating though this affliction was, what killed him in the end was, so to speak, the cure. In December 1906 he left Cambridge rather later than usual to join his family who had gone ahead to Las Palmas. On board ship he contracted influenza which the ship's doctor shamefully neglected, and he arrived in the Canaries delirious with double pneumonia. He died peacefully on 17 December 1906, having crowded into the fifty-six years of his life and the twenty-two of scholarly activity an amount that few achieve in twice that time.

Maitland's fame, it is agreeable to report, was not purely posthumous: recognition, richly deserved, came steadily in his last years. Five universities – not only Cambridge and Oxford and Glasgow (the hand of his friend George Neilson?), but also less expectedly Moscow (the hand of Vinogradoff!) and Cracow – bestowed honorary degrees. Both the Royal Prussian and the Royal Bavarian Academies elected him a corresponding member at an age unusually early for such distinctions, and he was one of the original fellows of the British Academy, founded two centuries too late in 1902. The institutions that had bred him recognized his stature – honorary fellow of Trinity, honorary bencher of Lincoln's Inn. Even eminent professors were not often in his day candidates for knighthood, which was just as well: 'Sir Frederic' would not have suited him, and he might, to his embarrassment, have felt obliged to decline if the offer had been made.

Though one feels at times that the study, writing and teaching of history must have totally absorbed all his waking time, he had, of course, a lot of other interests and concerns. We must never forget that he was by training a lawyer – no one trained him as a historian – even though what came to concern him about the law was its history. He had spent years in legal practice, though it must be conceded with little sign of ever becoming successful at it; at any rate, he was a markedly more knowledgeable lawyer than his father and grandfather had ever been. He held a chair of law, lectured regularly for the Law Tripos, and as a member of the Law Faculty made his presence felt in the University. This was one of his reasons for refusing the Regius chair of history when it was offered him in 1902 on Acton's death, though he mainly declined because he thought that the Regius professor 'is expected to speak to the world at large and even if I had anything to say to the W. at L. I don't think that I should like full houses and the limelight.'[22] Of his books only the little thing on *Justice and Police* says enough about the law rather than legal history to be assigned to that side of him, but he wrote a number of important papers on strictly legal matters in which his preference for history at most provided a setting. Such writings of his as those on the reform of the land law or on trusts, while they constantly testify to his awareness of the centuries which lay behind the conditions he was considering in his own day, are not contributions to legal history and must not concern us in the present discussion.[23] But Maitland was an unusual kind of lawyer which, since few have ever managed to hew close simultaneously to the principles of both law and history, is perhaps unsurprising.[24] Some of his work could be, and in consequence was, read as supporting the devotional adoration for the English common law which characterized English and American lawyers then and is still found widely practised. Maitland, on the other hand, regarded this law with a distaste only increased by his understanding how conditioned by history many of its absurdities were. He campaigned for the reform of the land law which would bring it into line with modern needs and concepts. He thought that it ought to shed those medieval and seventeenth-century relics which formed the substance of his daily labours, and which real lawyers loved because they helped to make them feel cosily safe and specially learned. Equity he regarded as particularly burdensome – 'at times I hate Equity and think of her as a short sighted busybody' – even though he had been 'bred in equity chambers and used to despise the common lawyer as an inferior person'.[25] But even so he spent much time on law and equity.

In late Victorian England a man's religion still mattered, and it was perhaps only in Cambridge that Maitland could get away with his position as a man who, as he once put it, dissented from all churches. He was in fact a figure increasingly typical during the last hundred years – Protestant by upbringing who had turned agnostic but retained a barely conscious Christian essence in his conduct and beliefs. Above all he abominated intolerance, testifying thus to an active scepticism which also prevented him from following his admired friend Sidgwick into the murky depths of spiritualism or, as the credulous liked to call it, Psychical Research. In politics Maitland opted naturally for the Liberal side, as any agnostic Cambridge utilitarian was bound to do, but his interest in such matters was lukewarm and intermittent. The Liberal split of 1886 left him with the unionist wing; the Boer War seriously distressed him and brought out his profound distrust of Joseph Chamberlain (a very conventional attitude); that politician's campaign for tariff reform returned Maitland to the Liberal party despite his contempt for Sir Henry Campbell-Bannerman.[26] Public affairs rarely appear in his correspondence: they seem to have interested him far less than the affairs of the University. He made no study of economics but like a good Liberal seems to have held an instinctive belief in free trade. He must have paid income tax but left no evidence of his doing so; if he had any views on Sir William Harcourt's introduction of death duties in 1894 he did not record them. In all this he was reasonably typical of a gentlemanly academic of his day, a body of men who, secure in the privileges of their institutions and contented with the adequate but by no means lavish income their positions provided, did not think politics particularly important.

Maitland was also fairly typical of his time and nation in loving music dearly, though unlike his wife he does not seem to have played any instrument; literature he liked well enough. Reading plea rolls and Year Books did not leave much time or room for other reading, but he was well brought up and well read: poetry and novels, especially the works of Walter Scott and Jane Austen, constituted a familiar part of his mental furniture, and this agnostic knew a lot of the Bible well enough for barely conscious quotations to appear in his writings. He discovered a passion for William Blake – perhaps the only fact about him that I find incomprehensible – and he came to dislike Kipling of whom he had 'enough and more than enough. I am inclined to think that he ought to have died young.'[27] Of course he read his fellow historians, such as Mandell Creighton and S. R. Gardiner (he wished Gardiner could write);[28] as his own work shows, he read an enormous amount of technical history in several languages. But he was also quite typical in what appears to have been a reasonable indifference to the fine arts; we hear nothing about painting or sculpture in his letters, though he had the conventional good eye for landscape on the ground. Most Englishmen and Englishwomen of the time got more from opera than from Michelangelo.

Deeply devoted to his family and firmly loyal to an ever increasing circle of friends, Maitland was at heart a very private man; even if there were any profit to be expected from investigating his psyche, common decency would forbid any such undertaking. So far as the signs go, he was a reasonably uncomplicated man of honour, good humour and general kindness. As is not unusual with private men, he used his wit to build his defences, though he rarely needed any. He was capable of using tiresomely coy phrases and in his correspondence with Pollock at times descended to some laboured jesting which, since it occurs nowhere else, probably reflects more upon Pollock than Maitland. When he got catty, which happened rarely, he confined his sarcasm to people whose public faces he did not think fully deserved – such men as the political theorist John Austin (whose work he abominated), Lord Acton (of whom his opinion improved by stages), Sir Henry Maine.[29] Somewhat frugal in eating and drinking, he approved of whisky.[30] When all is said and done, no reason can be found for dissenting from Fisher's verdict – 'a nature of singular charm and beauty'.

In the end we come to the real Frederic William Maitland, the historian who passed through the study of metaphysics and the law before he turned to history. History not only answered his search for an avocation but ruled his life and shaped his mind. So far did the historian triumph over the philosopher and lawyer that Maitland could tell Sidgwick, of all people, that 'inductive political science' (then the highly popular predecessor of the modern social sciences) is rubbish.[31] Indeed, he had thought so from the first: in the rather dreary reflections of his fellowship thesis it is quite a relief to come upon praise for the earl of Clarendon, who gave the historian's answer to Hobbes's 'practice of deciding historical and constitutional questions "by speculation and deduction"'.[32] It is a lesson that too many modern historians are at present trying to unlearn: they need their Maitland. Therefore, what sort of a historian was he?

2 The Historian

In Maitland's day historians, especially English historians, virtually never reflected on their activities. Most of them wrote history – or failed to commit their knowledge to paper – because they enjoyed doing so, and they did not feel called upon to philosophize about it; at most they would stake claims for the role their calling played in the formation of public men. Philosophers accepted the triumph of historical studies which had followed in the wake of the renewal of the methods of enquiry that in the course of the nineteenth century had spread from Germany to all of Europe. Sprung from the rise of romanticism and nationalism which had originated in the later eighteenth century, the dominance of historical studies as the best way to understand humanity was later reinforced by Darwinian theories of evolution which seemed to demonstrate that all creation rested on historical principles. True, other social studies were beginning to make themselves felt. Anthropology directed the influential, though in the end misleading, work of Sir Henry Maine, and theoretical sociology, operating by analysis of the present without much regard for roots and antecedents, began to make itself felt through such writers as Auguste Comte and Herbert Spencer. Nor was there much debate about methods in that positivist age: diligent reading of the sources, assisted by a conventional view of human nature (Freud had still to cast his baleful shadow) and plain common sense, was mostly regarded as adequate. Some historians went to the archives, as James Anthony Froude did; such others as Edward Augustus Freeman made do with what was in print. Guides to the student, full of the distillation of experience and over-methodizing everything, appeared in German and French, but not in English. The ideal goal was generally held to be the large, mainly narrative, description of a segment of time, of the past of a nation, or of such an institution as the papacy. William Stubbs, Regius professor at Oxford and afterwards bishop there, received special admiration because after years of labour devoted to the editing of chronicles he triumphantly produced his three volumes of the *Constitutional History of England* (1874–8). Stubbs drew his line at 1485, and indeed professionally respected history tended to be medieval. The search for origins, so powerful a stimulus to the historical studies of the seventeenth century, had revived in an age which regarded Victorian England as the outstanding culmination of a long development in human government, power and civilization.

Maitland distrusted generalizations, or rather the glibness with which large generalizations were made, and if he never wrote the 'great book' in the manner of Stubbs or Froude it was because he saw no point in doing so until historians had gone much more deeply into the sources. It is notable that this admirer of the German historians never pronounced the conventional encomium on Ranke which one finds scattered through much comment at the time; perhaps more surprisingly, he seems never to have encountered Jakob Burckhardt whose interest in the general history of civilization rather than politics he shared.[1] Most of his asides on history reveal only his genuine modesty about himself. He thought that he lacked the ability to write great books of the conventional kind, a performance he was content to leave to others. He expressed sincere admiration for Stubbs's achievement, even though he knew well enough that he was engaged in destroying many of the foundations of that Tory scholar's whiggish synthesis.[2]. And in spite of his philosophical training he rarely put thoughts on his concept of history on paper.

Only in his inaugural lecture, 'Why the History of English Law Remains Unwritten', did he come close to a statement of his credo.[3] He explained the absence of a history of the law in part by means of the isolated position occupied by lawyers: they who, unlike other scholars, could understand and use the materials were not interested in using them historically and never looked around at other forms of intellectual enterprise. Yet 'history involves comparison': the closed exploration of a single system cannot produce history. This is very true: much history always was and continues to be hampered by such isolation, and one of the chief virtues of historical studies lies in the breakdown of unconscious assumptions when they come up against alternative circumstances and convictions. Much of the impact of Maitland's work stood linked to his knowledge of the legal history of other countries. Furthermore, to him historical enquiry demanded the subversion of what had been said before: 'An orthodox history seems to me a contradiction in terms ... If we try to make history the handmaid of dogma she will soon cease to be history.' Another very true observation which a great many modern historians would do well to heed.

Such views arise in part from a naturally sceptical temperament (essential to the good historian) which questions everything until genuine proof is proffered, but in Maitland this inclination received reinforcement from his never ceasing awareness of the vast reservoir of historical materials that remained unexplored. Piled up in the archives, so far unread and even more commonly unedited, he saw the deposits of men's experience and deeds – not just the letters which most historians knew about but records legal, financial, economic, of men's thoughts: how could anyone understand an age without their use? How could one continue to write history out of chronicles, aided only by a few samples of those archives that happened to have been put into print? His understanding of the historian's labours was dominated by his awareness of those mountains of writs, rolls, accounts and so forth stored (mostly) at the Public Record Office, all waiting to be read and analysed. 'Hoarded wealth,' as he told his audience, which enjoyed the lecture but had no idea what the professor was talking about, 'yields no interest.'[4] He wished that wealth to be put in circulation.

The interest, he knew well enough, would not materialize in

constitutional histories (Stubbs) or narrative accounts of the Tudor age (Froude): 'Perhaps,' he cried out, 'there are countries in which the writing of historical monographs has become a nuisance; but surely it is better to have too many than none at all.'[5] When he said this there existed almost no monographs written by Englishmen about the history of their law and government; such work as had been done came from Germany and the United States. A year later, introducing a very learned account of 'The Materials for English Legal History', he recorded the words of 'a distinguished English lawyer' who was prepared to leave the writing of a history of English law to 'some of the antiquarian scholars of Germany and America' since Englishmen would lack 'the patience and learning to attempt it'.[6] Gentlemen at most write pretty little essays; they leave it to dull foreigners to get their hands dirty in the dust of the archives. As usual Maitland was too courteous to express the contempt for such attitudes which he clearly felt and which helped to fuel those twenty-odd years of feverish work on the sources.

One other remark in that inaugural lecture deserves attention here. Aware that one of the obstacles to good legal history lay in the lawyer's necessary preoccupation with the current meaning of the law, he stated 'that a thorough training in modern law is almost indispensable for anyone who wishes to do good work on legal history'.[7] That was probably truer in his day than it has since become; the many reforms of the last hundred years have terminated so much of the old law that present-day lawyers tend to be more bewildered by what they encounter in the middle ages or the sixteenth century than assisted by their legal expertise. But Maitland's reason was specific: the legal historian would 'often have to work from the modern to the ancient, from the clear to the vague, from the known to the unknown'. That method he was to employ particularly in *Domesday Book and Beyond*, but it can be traced through a great deal of his work. It has its dangers; it can harden the teleological attitudes and manners of reflection habitual with lawyers; we shall see that Maitland did not always escape them.[8] But he was right in thinking this way of proceeding frequently unavoidable as well as highly illuminating.

As Maitland always insisted, in the middle ages the materials of history were mainly the materials of the law; to him the history of the law constituted a preliminary step towards the history of medieval people in general. The accident of his training and the nature of the sources that captivated him thus took him into what some have called the narrow limits of legal history. The vast bulk (though by no means all of it) of medieval historical material is indeed the product of the law and its courts.[9] Maitland, however, understood what has not always been grasped so clearly since, namely that those records enshrine the lives of individuals and communities in all sorts of aspects – that properly understood they could be used to recover the real fullness of those lives. A short passage in his inaugural lecture in a way constitutes his own programme of work which even for the middle ages, not to mention later sectors of English history, remains uncompleted:[10]

Think for a moment what lies concealed within the hard rind of legal history. Legal documents, documents of the most technical kind, are the best, often the only evidence we have for social and economic history, for the history of morality, for the history of practical religion. Take a broad subject – the condition of the great mass of Englishmen in the later middle ages, the condition of the villagers. That might be pictured for us in all truthful detail; its political, social, economic, moral aspects might all be brought out; every tendency of progress or degradation might be traced; our supply of evidence is inexhaustible: but no one will extract its meaning who has not the patience to master an extremely formal system of pleading and procedure, who is not familiar with a whole scheme of actions with repulsive names. There are large and fertile tracts of history which the historian as a rule has to avoid because they are too legal.

The first part of this pronouncement – wise as well as exacting – has quite often been heeded by scholars who thought the second needlessly pernickety; very few have brought to the use of legal records in the search for history other than legal that understanding of the law which alone unlocks the records. Maitland did. Yet examples still abound of the errors lurking in wait for those who think that the materials of the law, especially when in print, can be understood by common sense; and those errors get aggravated when scholars commit the other sin condemned by Maitland – when history is made to serve dogma.[11] Legal records are indeed a repository of knowledge stretching far beyond the reconstruction of the history of law, but they cannot well be used by the ignorant and innocent. However, as Maitland knew and said, that means only that the ignorant should learn, the innocent grow wise, not that the records should be left unstudied.

Thus Maitland in effect declared that in the first instance the historian must grasp the law that produced those records, which means the law of that day in its own right and operation. This comprehension determined his evident strategy: he needed to understand before he could write. In consequence, a great part of the corpus of his work consists of preparatory labours leading up to the coping stone of either a genuine synthesis or at least a powerful suggestion how the synthesis will come out. This is a manner of proceeding which only a man of his phenomenal speed and memory can afford to practise if those coping stones are ever to be reached. His astounding capacity for holding things in the mind also appears in his obedience to his own dictum that history calls for comparisons. Maitland not infrequently described himself as ignorant of other laws and other countries, and no doubt by the side of his knowledge of the common law his understanding of other systems looked pale. However, his work, and especially his footnotes, contradict these well-meant expressions of modesty. In his discussion, for instance, of 'The Early History of Malice Aforethought', an essay published as early as 1883, he showed himself well acquainted with the laws of

Germany and France; a later paper on the esoteric theme 'Possession for Year and Day' displayed a special knowledge of the ancient laws of those countries.[12] Evidence abounds of his enormously wide reading in several languages: there are a good few scholars of his day who would now be totally forgotten but for their appearance in his footnotes. The author of *Roman Canon Law in the Church of England* knew a great deal about that system, and although the book did not appear until 1898 it included essays written as early as 1886. Maitland knew enough of it – of its sources and its implications – to understand why the high-church men of his own day thought it wiser to cultivate their ignorance of it.[13] As for the civil or Roman law, though he regularly professed himself to be but indifferently learned in it and certainly never acquired a full mastery, he knew its sources and could direct others to the right books: he knew it better than he thought or said.[14] He no sooner made the acquaintance of a Scots lawyer than he eagerly enquired after the old law of that country.[15] No man more diligently struggled to avoid the insularity of the common law; much of the enduring strength of his learning derives from his well-instructed ability to see the history of that law three-dimensionally in a world which held those other laws as well.

The mainstay of that strength, however, lay in his determination really to understand his sources – their contents and their limitations. Though he never explained his working methods they jump from the page as one reviews his labours. London was in his day probably a little more accessible from Cambridge than it is now, but even so there were problems of distance and travel, especially in a busy term time. But Maitland spent a great many hours – sometimes any spare moment he could snatch from other engagements in the capital – at the Public Record Office; quite manifestly, as casual remarks show, he saw a very wide range of manuscripts from feet of fines and plea rolls to letters patent and state papers, some of which never got used in his writings. He had an advantage over the present day: at that time the P.R.O.

attracted few people and produced documents at enviable speed. True, the two fat volumes of *The History of English Law* appear to rest entirely on records in print (listed at the start in three and a half crowded pages), but – apart from the fact that a knowledge of unprinted and uncited manuscripts lay behind much that was said – quoting only print was made possible in great part by his own previous editorial labours – especially *Bracton's Note-Book, Memoranda de Parliamento*, and several Selden Society volumes. His edition of the *Note-Book* – identified by him as the collection of cases on which the author of that famous thirteenth-century treatise rested his description of the law of England – constituted his major breakthrough to an understanding of the treatise itself; and this remains crucial even if we have to think him mistaken, as shortly we shall see he was, about both Bracton and the *Note-Book*. What matters here is the manner of working – from the sources, through preliminary labours to the great work. Maitland's lesser writings frequently combine the character of research programmes with the preliminary sorting out of problems; and one reason for his long influence lies in the fact that he himself was not given the time to follow up all the lines he opened.

The story of Maitland's long love affair with the Year Books is instructive. Like every other lawyer with an interest in history, he knew, of course, about these collections of cases put together annually from about the reign of Edward I onwards. That is to say, he was familiar with the mainly pretty poor editions in black-letter, published in the sixteenth century. He revelled in their immediacy and reality – the record of arguments and discussion in court, of *obiter dicta* and jokes and (rarely) grounds given for decisions. He also knew their serious shortcomings – texts often corrupted and contents quite insufficiently explained. Then on Wednesday, 21 April 1886, he was approached by Henry Maxwell Lyte (deputy keeper of the public records, then the title of the head of the P.R.O.) with the suggestion that the Year Books needed a modern edition. This would in fact appear to have been the first personal contact between the two men. By Saturday Maitland had thought the problem through to the point of being able to submit a full-scale programme of editing and publication, a programme which he then found himself committed to initiating in person.[16] The surviving volumes for Edward I had already been edited, very poorly, for the Rolls Series (1866–79), while an encouraging start had been made in the same series on the reign of Edward III. Maitland therefore proposed to tackle the extensive collection for Edward II. He asked to be allowed to wait until he had finished *Bracton's Note-Book*, but in fact a great many other engagements intervened before, in 1903, he was able to produce his first Year Book edition. However, when at last he found time for the task he not only produced a model edition but prefaced it with another of those preparatory exercises he knew to be essential to a true understanding: he reconstructed at length the grammar and vocabulary of the medieval Law-French in which the Books were written. Since the use of this specialized jargon had been abolished by statute in 1731, understanding of it had become a lost art: only Maitland's remarkable excursus into philology made the proper use of those invaluable materials possible.[17]

In his introduction the editor further settled the real character of the Year Books (a point he himself had still been uncertain about even two years earlier): he showed them to have been students' compilations made from notes in court, and not, as had been supposed on ancient authority, semi-official collections of cases made for the use of judges and counsel. At the same time he set out the arguments for their use by historians in ways that have become classic. Here, as he told us, we find the living language and practice of the law – a guide not only to the law but to the very life of the nation. I think myself that, though he was on the right lines, his enthusiasm exaggerated the profit likely to be got from that source: it does tell us more about law than about life. Even so, Maitland's enthusiasm helps to explain why he never continued writing the history of English law beyond the reign of Edward I. No one was more convinced than he that this could not be done until the Year Book material had been properly digested, which meant first properly edited. It added a whole new dimension to the sources available to the legal historian, enabling him to see the law in operation and not only as defined in edicts or collected in codes. He himself edited two more volumes in the three remaining years of his life, the last brought out after his death by G. J. Turner, whose combination of fine scholarship and indolence had often driven Maitland to distraction. For a while the Selden Society's Year Book series continued active, and from 1914 the Ames Foundation at Harvard joined in with editions for Richard II's reign. But the gaps remain enormous: twenty-three volumes now cover only the first twelve of Edward II's twenty regnal years, and we have only three volumes edited for Richard II's twenty-two, not to mention the bare sprinkling of volumes for the fifteenth century. The drive behind the editing of Year Books has slackened: it is widely held that a man can do more important work and earn a greater repute by less laborious exercises. Yet it is true that Maitland diagnosed their value pretty correctly and that they remain underused.[18]

Thus equipped, Maitland tackled the task of writing real history. Reading the sources properly and solving their problems may seem so obvious a preparatory stage that it hardly deserves so much comment. It is nothing of the sort: great reputations have been made, both before Maitland's day and after, by men who fudged both the reading and the analysis of their sources; because Maitland was a medievalist, it has proved easier for this state of affairs to endure in the post-medieval period. The strength behind Maitland's astounding endurance lay in the fact that – instinctively, it seems, for he had no guide or model – he chose to work correctly. Another source of that strength, however, may be found in his careful restriction of his area of operations. Maitland wrote so much, nearly all of it of genuine importance, that one can forget his decision to limit himself in time. Not for him the writing of sixteen volumes covering all the history of English law from Anglo-Saxon times to 1875, which remarkable achievement Sir William Holdsworth produced solely out of printed materials. (It is said that he saved time by never taking a note but worked at his desk at All Souls, surrounded by terraces of books with marking slips in them.) Not for Maitland either the often slender and sometimes credulous foundation of evidence and interpretation employed by Holdsworth, whose great work has for years been as much an obstacle as an aid to the correct understanding of the themes he treated. Maitland was, in effect, content to be the historian of English law from the Conquest to the reign of Edward I – quite a sufficient era to study from the sources, in all conscience. Of course, he did extend his range on occasion – back into pre-Conquest England, or into the fifteenth century for the canon law, or less successfully into the supposed Renaissance of the sixteenth – but in the main he stayed with the ages of Glanvill and Bracton which it was his achievement to show forth as the formative and decisive era in the history of the common law.

There was another limitation in his method which assisted the concrete definition and solidity of his work but does not seem to have been noticed before. Though many of his essays, particularly the earlier ones before he fully realized the nature of his sources, ranged across stretches of time and varieties of materials, his great books took their origin from concentration on one particular source, usually an ancient treatise. The method recalls the principle of the old 'readings' at the Inns of Court for which the lecturer chose a single statute and built up his exposition of the law by tracking developments upon one section after another through the subsequent case-law. *The History of English Law* ('Pollock and Maitland') took its origin from a study of the treatise ascribed to Henry de Bracton; it is not without significance that the section on pre-Norman England was Pollock's sole contribution. *Domesday Book and Beyond* announces the principle in its title: an analysis of Domesday Book was used to extrapolate law and society backwards, from (as Maitland had advised in his inaugural lecture) the known to the unknown. The treatise on the canon law contained, as already mentioned, a collection of essays on various aspects of the subject, but its core consisted of a study of William Lyndwood's fifteenth-century *Provinciale*. In his Ford lectures at Oxford, *Township and Borough*, the single book was replaced by the single town, and a pretty small one at that: he used medieval Cambridge to recreate the realities of medieval urban and rural conditions. It may be doubted whether any other great historian ever so regularly received inspiration from a restricted and restricting source, only to burst out of it by pursuing the suggestions he found there into a whole range of sources and problems. The method helps to explain Maitland's astonishing productivity. Concentrate a well-stocked mind upon a single compilation, apply to it the kind of precise reasoning and concrete imagination Maitland possessed, and useful, even powerful, results will come forth far more rapidly than they do to the historian who reads a whole body of source materials with a mind to finding out what actually happened. Both are thorough, but one starts from inspiration and the other from perspiration – not a new crack, I know, but distinctly apposite here. Maitland's ability to discern patterns of existence and development – that skill with which he rapidly ordered an inchoate mass of details, and which has convincingly been linked to his training as a lawyer[19] – owed a great deal to his habit of working outwards from a central source.

Maitland's skill in producing a convincing shape of the past is the more remarkable because he in effect avoided the most common and most traditional of expository schemes. He wrote no, or almost no, narrative, and he regarded himself as incapable of telling a story in the usual manner. When during the planning of *The History of English Law* Pollock tried to persuade him to write a short outline history of that law at least covering the middle ages, Maitland retorted with an explanation of his approach to the writing of history.[20] He himself, he said, could not forget the many problems which ignorance placed in the way of the treatment proposed: he needed to analyse and dispose of them first. But he encouraged Pollock to go ahead and write 'a famous book'. He could not pass over complex issues 'in a few brief paragraphs – if I am to write about it I can not but write at length.' 'I quite see that a brief history of English law is much wanted and might be written, but I also see that I can not write it.' He did actually change his mind sufficiently to produce eighty pages of such 'Outlines of English Legal History, 560–1600' for a once famous collection of essays on English social history.[21] Its author, were he not known, is unmistakable on every page, but the sum total leaves a good deal to be desired. Episodic and epigrammatical, it solves far fewer of the problems along the road than it seems to think, and once Maitland leaves his familiar stamping ground to look at the fifteenth and sixteenth centuries he loses most of his sovereignty. His accounts, for instance, of Parliament and Star Chamber, though they contain some of his typical flashes of insight, are really caricatures. This happened because here Maitland was of necessity forced to rely on other people's views which he had not had the time to test against the sources: where he happens to know some piece of evidence properly he at once corrects vulgar error, but this happens rarely in that gallant, and misconceived, survey.

Thus analysis, not narrative, constituted Maitland's organizing principle for the writing of history. His admiration for Stubbs, he said, grew every day, and with that model of the long narrative before him he felt quite unable to think of emulating it.[22] He really did not believe that he could write continuous narrative. Now in a way this is absurd: no one could tell a story better than Maitland, as his daughter (among others) testified.[23] *The History of English Law* teems with brief tales that transform abstract analysis into the living experience of real people. Take just one example, the explanation of the survival in Kent of the peculiar custom known as gavelkind (partiple inheritance among male heirs).[24] Where others might have laboriously set out the law of this exception

31

to the rule and perhaps speculated about the endurance of ancient custom, Maitland in two pages written in the present tense brings the men of Kent – tenants as well as lords – vividly before us in what is in effect a tale of their dealings with one another, and by the end we understand why gavelkind survived there at a time when primogeniture was sweeping the board everywhere else. Thus if Maitland really believed himself to be incapable of narrative history he was wrong; it was his purpose – his determination to understand and explain before he told – not his deficiencies that pointed the way to essentially analytical techniques. His disavowals should perhaps be read in the context of his time. While narrative nowadays ranks rather low in the estimation of professional historians, in the age of Stubbs and Froude, of Freeman and Gardiner the notion that real historians tell great (and lengthy) stories still prevailed. This was not the only aspect of professional history in which Maitland proved himself to be the first of the moderns.

Maitland's method has its dangers which shall be discussed in a moment. But in the first place it made Maitland into the enduring writer of history that he became. The history he wrote concerned itself with highly technical issues and used materials and terms of art that are not accessible to the general reader; indeed, too few historians have bothered to master them since. In Maitland's hands they created lasting orthodoxies. The age of Henry II as the foundation era of settled government and the common law; the age of Bracton as the era of codification and consolidation, as English custom underwent scrutiny by eyes trained in the law of Rome; the lore of the forms of action as the essence of medieval jurisprudence; the analysis of society in terms of tenures; the discovery of Anglo-Saxon social and economic arrangements by working backwards from 1086; the medieval Parliament as a court rather than a political assembly; the dominance of papal law in the English church down to the Reformation; the vital significance of the Year Books – all these and many more commonplaces of our understanding of the English middle ages were created in Maitland's two decades of almost feverish activity. A hundred years of teaching have anchored them in concrete so well set that every effort of doubt or modification calls for dynamite.

Once Maitland had found his vocation he treated it as a solemn duty which, being the most unsolemn of men, he somewhat shamefacedly admitted he enjoyed enormously. When he assured the editors of a technical collection of legal cases that they had given him hours of unalloyed pleasure, we believe him literally where with anyone else we might suspect hypocrisy; his book on the canon law, he said, brought him more fun than 'any other job I ever did'.[25] In fact, that he enjoyed himself all the time both researching and writing springs from just about every page he wrote. This is among historians by no means a common experience, even among the active sector of the profession; far more of them will recognize the truth of A. F. Pollard's remark about 'the toil of producing research which it is only a pleasure to pursue'. Maitland enjoyed both the seeking of the truth – in materials immensely more difficult and indeed repellent than Pollard, careful avoider of manuscripts, ever studied – and the telling of it.

A striking irony lies embedded in Maitland's long ascendancy over the territory which he not only made his own but also persuaded others to regard as the central region of medieval history. The man who declared that an orthodox history was a contradiction in terms created despite himself an orthodoxy so enduring that even his latter-day critics speak as though in the presence of a god whose wrath might still strike them down. We have no English historian before him whose work is still treated as though it was the latest, even the last, word, and among his immediate successors only T. F. Tout and a little later Sir Frank Stenton are still read for the serious, by now much criticized, content of their books. Sir Charles Firth, A. F. Pollard, Sir Maurice Powicke, Sir Lewis Namier, Sir John Neale (knighthoods came to historians after Maitland's day), all great names once and still respected for what once they did: but no one refers to them as though despite their tiresome departure to the grave they were living colleagues and fellow-workers. That is how we treat Maitland. Some on that list – especially the last two – actually wished to create orthodoxies and enduring truths. They failed where Maitland, modestly unconvinced that final answers are possible for historians, became an oracle whose sayings, it seems, do enshrine such impossible truths. Why?

Some points are obvious but also rather superficial. There is the manifest fact that Maitland knew what he was talking about, had done a vast deal of work, and seemed always able to distinguish speculation from certainty. Criticizing Maitland has in part proved so difficult because of the caution with which he formulated his answers, a caution not at first apparent in the transparent lucidity of his style. However, there were two very special reasons which assisted in the prolonged survival of his work. In his own line, he has never until very recently had numerous successors, able to take up his questions and his sources, and able to develop his themes beyond the point to which he had taken them. And secondly, he wrote better than any serious historian of England has ever done, before or since his time. It is virtually impossible to be bored by Maitland even at his most technical, and seeing how very boring even good historians can be this gives him a remarkable advantage. Without any intention of playing the advocate, he insensibly persuades, even enslaves, by the beauty of his style. These two points need a little more analysis.

Why have there been so few historians of the law – real historians of quality, I mean? For a time it seemed as though only one of rank was to be permitted to every generation, the staff passing, after an interval, from Maitland to Theodore Plucknett (*difficilis descensus* . . .?) and then to Samuel Thorne, though of late the great revival of legal history has at last picked up the message and inspiration of Maitland. This has led to a major extension of the territory covered by sound legal history and almost inevitably has brought with it the discovery that even Maitland needs revising, at the periphery and in the centre. By real historians of the law I mean scholars who can satisfy both historians and lawyers that they understand their themes. Maitland's inaugural lecture proves that he knew the fundamental problem well enough. Practitioners and historians concern themselves with the same body of materials, but in it they seek totally different things.

A lawyer finds on his table a case about rights of common which sends him to the Statute of Merton. But is it really the law of 1236 he wants to know? No, it is the ultimate result of the interpretations set on the statute by the judges of twenty generations . . . What the lawyer wants is authority and the newer the better; what the historian wants is evidence and the older the better.[26]

No two breeds of learned men differ more widely in their acquired mental characteristics, and the accident that they operate on the same sources disguises the essential irreconcilability of their concerns. I have always found it much easier to understand the thought processes of physicists or biologists, analysing their problems empirically, than those of lawyers seeking guidance for present action from decisions and sayings whose very words have quite probably changed their meaning several times over the centuries. Their circumstances certainly have. The lawyers' teleological preoccupation, in which all things past have meaning only insofar as they can be shown to have led to a present use, beset English history for centuries: historians were led to believe that their task lay in explaining the present rather than the past.[27]

The distance between minds that wish to know what seven centuries have made of the Statute of Merton, and those who wish to know what the makers of the statute thought they were doing, is so great as to be ordinarily unbridgable. Men who have an instinctive grasp of the law and its ways stand at the opposite end of the spectrum from men who have an instinctive grasp of the past and its ways. Yet, as Maitland understood and demonstrated, the medieval past and its ways have mainly to be reconstructed from sources produced by the law and its operation. Small wonder that a true historian who can cope with the law of the past is a rare thing, even though I could now name a dozen who have really learned to tie the ends of the spectrum together; small wonder that an exceptional historian like Maitland, who to the uncommon double skill added wonderful gifts as a scholar and writer, found himself elevated to a plinth on which the word *veritas* was engraven by generations of admirers.

As for Maitland's style, much has been written about it, most of it true. It combines earnestness and wit, charm and sinew, in a manner so personal that any attempt to learn from it would be idiocy. We are often warned not to imitate Maitland, and no one has ever seriously tried to do so, but it has to be confessed that a solid diet of reading Maitland does have its effects. All of a sudden one finds oneself using the first person plural (one of Maitland's most obtrusive hallmarks), starting sentences with 'Now, . . . ', introducing concrete metaphors by way of explanation. Maitland, in his innocence, works insidiously. Yet resistance is very necessary; more than most historians, Maitland testifies to the truth that the style is the man. Those usually short, often vibrating, sentences, the avoidance of learned circumlocutions and even long words as such; the manner in which the royal 'we' gathers the reader into the company of the writer; the constant illumination of abstract or general notions by anchoring them in the experience of real people; the frequent (possibly unconscious) echoes from a whole cultural reservoir filled with, among other things, the Bible; the wit which, because it grows naturally from the discourse, remains funny to this day; and the courtesy which renders the not infrequent stabs of the stiletto painless: all these compass Maitland the man, a man both wise and artless. It seems that Maitland was in no sense a conscious stylist, a careful and particular carpenter of words and architect of sentences: nobody who wrote so much so fast could have been. True, he wrote even his lectures out in full and practised them before delivery, a delivery which depended upon the presence of a script. This might argue against spontaneity and for painful labour, but the conclusion would be false. Indeed, it is rather that Maitland's manner of lecturing explains his style: whether speaking or writing, he was always talking to the reader as much as to a listener. It is because his written words bring the sound of his voice even to generations that could never hear him that he remains so alive, so immediate, so insidious a writer.

One genre of writing, rarely commented on in thinking about Maitland, will help to explain further. One of the duties of the learned is to review the work of others, and Maitland did a certain amount of this: not all that much because what in his wake was to become a flood of medieval monographs, in his own day was still but a trickle. Still, he wrote a number of notices all of which show the same characteristics: generous acknowledgment of the reviewed author's attainment, plain but courteous correction of error, and an elegant conciseness. Models of their kind, in a way, for reviews must neither evade the duty to advance the state of scholarship nor do so with savagery, but as a rule a bit anodyne. Once, however, Maitland removed the baffles. He was reviewing John Horace Round's *The Commune of London and Other Studies* (1899), and he felt obliged to speak out about that sinister, touchy and quarrelsome controversialist's manner and defects. The result was a unique piece of learning mixed with invective, the more devastating because it spoke quietly, with irony and a touch of condescension.[28] It shows what Maitland could do when really roused. He took Round to task for never producing a real book but only collections of disparate papers, a habit which, Maitland said, gave grounds unhappily to those who thought that serious research stood in the way of writing history, and he topped this by citing Renan's remark that no one can be at one and the same time a good controversialist and a good historian. Then he cut loose. Round had made a nasty crack about a minor error of Kate Norgate's to the effect that 'one must not be severe on a lady's Latin'; finding a German name misspelt in the book before him did not, said Maitland, make him point out that the author's 'acquaintance with the German tongue is but gentlemanly'. Round, still pursuing his endless feud with the long-dead Freeman, referred to a little *clique* of Oxford historians who had 'endeavoured, without scruple and with almost unconcealed anger, to silence me at any cost'; 'they must be simple folk down there at Oxford,' said Maitland, 'to think that Mr Round will ever be silent' about his own rightness and the wrongs committed by his adversaries. Round's whine that 'in England, at the present, there is neither inducement nor reward' for original research calls forth the retort that anyone writing in Round's antiquarian fashion must expect to remain unread by the general public: 'We know of no country in the world where there is any pressing demand for short studies of disconnected themes.' And on he went to dissect the book, mixing open admiration for its excellences with precise critique of its deficiencies. As Maitland should have expected, the review caused deep offence, and what had been a quite regular correspondence between the two eminent scholars came to an end. Maitland foresaw 'that I shall now have J.H.R. as an assailant for our joint lives'.[29] But it is plain that he had no regrets. He abominated Round's manners, which he had had occasion to deplore before when Round had attacked the misfortunate Hubert Hall, a scholar who had invited the tiger-cat's assault by producing a far from perfect edition: 'If all that R. says is true, I still think that he is using language which should be reserved for cases of a different sort . . . Poor Hall has a fluffy mind but never scamps work, besides being (but this alas is irrelevant) the most unselfish man I have ever known.'[30] Maitland evidently thought Round's behaviour intolerable in a fellow scholar, and when finally provoked said so. It was in fact virtually impossible to live in the same world as Round without causing him in the end to take offence: to him, the taking of offence was the elixir of life. He who had hitherto flattered Maitland 'absurdly'[31] no doubt felt particularly shattered by an attack from that quarter, but I think that Maitland enjoyed the opportunity to execute justice on a persistent offender. I certainly hope he did.

Maitland's greatness and the elements that went to the making of it should thus not be doubted. However, it is no service to him to turn admiration into adulation. It was no service to his own convictions to set him up for orthodoxy and for decades to cite him as scripture. He never believed himself to be a god or even to be humanly perfect in his ways, and we should not evade the duty to say something about the weaknesses or errors that may – are bound to – accompany his transcendent skills. In the last twenty years or so, a good deal of his work has at last been accorded the honour of proper criticism; at last his unwanted orthodoxy has gone, leaving behind his true achievement, to be assessed in the historian's manner which he wished to teach to others.

There have before this been attempts to evaluate Maitland's work against revisions and departures since his day; they have been marked by a careful listing of changing views and all avoidance of the possible reasons why Maitland, so formidably persuasive in his judgments, might here or there have erred.[32] They have also usually and rightly recognized that Maitland's habitual caution allowed him to qualify even very positive assertions in such a way as to prepare the road for his revisers.[33] I shall confine myself to some major issues, taking it for granted that a century of research will bring with it some modifications here and there.[34]

The 'garrison theory' of the origin of English boroughs (that they started as places fortified against Danish invaders), a theory he put forward in *Domesday Book and Beyond* as well as in *Township and Borough*, and which his disciples came to overwork, was criticized in a famous review by James Tait who then took some forty years to bring out his definitive, and very soporific, statement on the matter.[35] Maitland, it is clear, underestimated the part which trade and merchants played in the rise of towns; he never proved himself more the lawyer than in his relative neglect of economic influences. Maitland's disparaging judgment of the law-book called *Fleta* (compiled early in the fourteenth century) – 'an edition of Bracton much abridged and "brought up to date" by references to the earlier

statutes of Edward I'[36] – has been thoroughly overthrown by
H. G. Richardson and G. O. Sayles (Maitland worshippers) in
their edition of that work.[37] Maitland's conviction that
Domesday Book was what he called a 'geld-book' – a register
of potential payers of the tax called danegeld – arose mainly
from the state of Domesday studies in his day; it has been
proved to be both wrong and seriously misleading.[38] Errors of
that kind, in themselves inevitable, do affect a historian's
general interpretation both of the sources and of the history he
gets from them, but they do not affect the greatness of
Maitland's achievement over all, nor did those critics suppose
that they did. Here I shall also omit a discussion of the one
work which has been almost universally rejected – Maitland's
Rede lecture on *English Law and the Renaissance*, which shall
receive proper attention in the next chapter. But there remain
three issues which seem to reach further and deserve a closer
look: Maitland's teaching on writs and the forms of action;
Maitland's assessment of Bracton; and Maitland's analysis of
the law of the twelfth century.

Maitland in effect taught us that the system of writs by
means of which actions were started constituted the essential
structure of the medieval law. This interpretation seemed to be
directly derived from the compendia produced at the time:
both the commentators (Glanvill, Bracton and so forth) and
the practitioners (in the so-called Register of Writs) built their
analysis of the law around these forms of action.[39] In this law
of procedure Maitland identified the predominant jurisprudence of the middle ages; as he once said, the medieval law
reversed the natural course of justice, for whereas justice
demands that for every wrong there shall be a remedy, the
middle ages held that where there is no remedy no wrong has
been committed. If there is no writ appropriate to a complaint,
the complainant can have no recourse to the law. It matters
little that he was wrong to doubt the existence of an 'official'
Register kept in the Chancery[40] or did not give sufficient place
to the history of the judicial writ before the age of Henry II:[41]
those are the normal details of disputable research. The former

mistake stemmed from the fact that Maitland did not have as large a sample of versions of the Register at his disposal as did later scholars; the second from his excessive respect for Henry II and relative ignorance of both Anglo-Saxon England and pre-Conquest Normandy. In both instances, the correctors acknowledge his inspiration. They would also do well to admire his far-seeing caution: thus a page in *The History of English Law* leaves the door wide open for the sort of revision since carried out by R. van Caenegem.[42]

Of far greater importance is the fact that Maitland ignored the plaint by bill, the bringing of an action not by original writ but by a form of petition in which the plaintiff could set out his grievance and pray for remedy. This, of course, made it possible for any alleged sufferer of a wrong to approach the king's court in search of justice, and indeed some of the forms of action owed their development to the provision of new remedies for wrongs raised by bill. Maitland knew this but the growing reluctance of Chancery to make new writs persuaded him to suppose that actions by bill disappeared from the courts and the common law not later than about the end of the fourteenth century as the Register of Writs settled into a final and immutable form; he held that in the later middle ages actions by bill belonged solely to the chancellor's court.[43] This may be true of Common Pleas but it is not true for the law at large. Not only was procedure by plaint freely used in the reign of Henry III;[44] it remained available in the King's Bench to the end of the middle ages and beyond.[45] Its willingness to hear plaintiffs by bill as well as by writ enabled that court to recover from the late-medieval slump in business that it experienced and to take over much litigation that earlier would have gone to other courts.[46]

More surprising than this failure to remember the bill was Maitland's treatment of trespass. Here, too, his understanding of the Register obscured his vision. Trespass troubled medieval lawyers by not fitting too well into any of their established categories. Here was a civil remedy for wrongs not very different from the crimes pursuable at the crown's suit. Its peculiarities are well summed up in the fact that unlike other forms of action it could command an enforcement procedure which culminated in outlawry, a means otherwise reserved to pleas of the crown (felonies). The lawyers' inability to cope with trespass lay at the heart of the deplorable underdevelopment of the medieval criminal law. Maitland saw the writ bobbing about the Register like a homeless waif, now accommodated here and now farmed out there, and he thus called it an intruder still not properly at home in the law by the end of the sixteenth century.[47] And he had virtually nothing to say about its offspring, trespass on the case, or simply case. Yet as a practitioner at the bar he must have been well aware that such actions as assumpsit (the basis of contract law) or trover (the basis of fraudulent conversion) stemmed from case, and he should have seen that in the fifteenth century case opened the law to new actions almost as freely as procedure by bill had done. In his lectures to students of the law he came very close to saying it all.[48] But he failed to draw the inferences. By ignoring bills and playing down case, Maitland for generations convinced historians that the late-medieval common law had 'ossified', so that it needed action by new courts (Chancery, Star Chamber) as well as Parliament to supply litigants with chances of redress in much altered circumstances. As we shall see, he thus totally missed one of the most remarkable events in the history of the common law as it renewed itself from within in response to need.[49] The fundamental cause of this mixture of error and blindness would seem to have lain in his trust in the Register of Writs as an authoritative and complete statement of the law.

The problem of Henry de Bracton, supposed author of the great treatise ascribed in Maitland's day to about the middle of the thirteenth century, is highly complex, and a brief summary must distort its subtleties.[50] Bracton was central to Maitland's work: an inspiration and guide whose book he knew inside out. One of his greatest feats of historical research produced the three-volume edition of what he called *Bracton's Note-Book*, a collection of cases which he identified as Bracton's source-book for his treatise. The reconstruction seemed the more convincing because Maitland found some of the cases so collected marked for transcription on the plea rolls. Maitland also convinced himself that though the author of the treatise had some acquaintance with the law of Rome he was insufficiently learned in it to have used it for the systematizing of English law: thus the ordered and advanced state of the law described in Bracton implied a highly developed achievement for the native law of England. Of all this very little now stands. The destroyer has been one of Maitland's greatest admirers, Samuel E. Thorne of Harvard University, who gave twenty years of his life to a final edition and accurate translation of 'Bracton'.[51] Thorne has demonstrated that the treatise as we have it did not come from one hand; several 'redactors' (whose existence Maitland had tentatively allowed for) had been at work on it and the text handed down to us was produced after the accession of Edward I in 1272 (Bracton died in 1268). Thorne has also shown it to be much more likely that the original work of collecting and collating was not done by the Henry of tradition but either by his master and teacher, William Ralegh, or by Ralegh's own revered mentor, Martin of Pateshull: a splendid trinity of leading judges in direct personal descent. The *Note-Book*, as Thorne shows, bears a far more distant relation to the contents of 'Bracton' than Maitland supposed, and the famous marginal notes on the plea rolls belong to many hands and possibly several centuries. Furthermore, and perhaps most to the detriment of the story as told by Maitland, Thorne has proved that those common-law judges knew the Roman *Code* very well, and that such order and system as they could manage to provide for the law of their own country derived from Rome. As for the law of England revealed in the treatise, it has turned out to lack system, to be often internally contradictory, and so to fall well short of the excellence discerned by Maitland. Some of that inadequacy, however, may well have been introduced by those later redactors who seem to have managed to muddle their predecessors' acquaintance with the Roman law as much as they introduced confusion into the law of England.

Now Thorne, who for some years after he published these formidable findings used to wear a button in his coat that read 'Bracton Lives', would be distressed if it were thought that he had in some way dethroned Maitland. On the contrary, his admiration for his predecessor remains undimmed, and he is more conscious than anyone of the care Maitland took to qualify his judgments when he knew he stood on shaky ground. Nevertheless, this recent history of Bracton's book amounts to more than ordinary revision in the course of advancing research. It is a major upheaval. We still await what may become of it all, but it looks to me as though much of the beautiful clarity of 'Pollock and Maitland', the apparent perfection of logic and sense upon which the iron grip of the work has rested, may well shatter as the lesson is absorbed that this supposedly comprehensive statement of English law 'in the age of Bracton' is instead a complex mixture of sense and doubts, a cumulated and only partially digested corpus strung along the only available lines of order, namely those confounded forms of action. Maitland had to use the printed form of Bracton produced in 1569 and reprinted with defects in 1640; he knew very well how inadequate this was and several times called for a new edition. Considering what he had to work with, his achievement remains astounding. That is not in question: what must now be asked is whether the product resulting from such handicaps can really, a hundred years after its appearance, still dominate all studies of English law in the middle ages.

This question is raised in its starkest form by the latest scholar to take his axe to the forest oak. Van Caenegem, Sayles, Thorne all remained and remain devotees of Maitland, even though they have found him wanting in some very important ways. Our last critic, however, though he too remains respectful and is liable to emphasize the temerity of his heretical views, has found real chinks in Maitland's armour. This is S. F. C. Milsom, who very appropriately practises legal history from a chair in Maitland's own university and like Maitland began his career as a lawyer.[52] The matters at issue turn upon highly technical points of the law and its record, and Milsom does not make things easier by an allusive and elliptical style, but they reach right down into our view of medieval society. The essence of his revisionist attack lies in his allegation that Maitland failed to give proper weight to the social structure of a feudal or seigneurial world: he overestimated the governing control of the king's courts and undervalued the independence of the local lords' courts. As Maitland saw it, Henry II's legislation (if that is what it was) replaced feudalism by centralized government when he offered better and swifter justice to complainants disturbed in their rights of possession by, as it were, interlopers; he identified seisin – the thing complainants sought to protect or recover – as equal to possession vested in them by grant or inheritance. In his world there were two contestants at law – he who claimed the land and he who sat on it – fighting out the rights of it before a relatively impartial court; unable to get what they held to be their just rights they took advantage of the king's offer in what Maitland called the possessory assizes (especially the assizes of novel disseisin and of mort d'ancestor) to help them to a solution of their problems. The picture Maitland drew of that world had a beautiful coherence and consistency, but it was the world as it emerged in his thirteenth-century sources read backwards and extended into the very different age that went before.

Milsom, on the other hand, argues for what he calls a three-dimensional world in which claimant, tenant (he who happens to hold at the relevant point in time) and lord are all involved in every such dispute, a world in which seisin is not a quality settled in the occupier of the land but an action of the lord's who invests another with seisin and thus at his pleasure makes him the rightful occupier for the time being.[53] Originally seisin was not equal to the concept of possession in the Roman law,

45

as Maitland maintained (and as in due course it became), but
the definition of a relationship created by the lord when he
admits another to hold land of him. The assizes are not
'possessory', a term that Maitland invented for them,[54] and
are not primarily intended to transfer actions to the king's
court; they are means for restoring the proper course of the
tenant's rights by urging the lord to do justice and not to abuse
his power. When the king's writ instructed the sheriff to see to
it that a dispute was settled by the lord it meant precisely that;
the ancillary sanction – if the lord refuses have the parties
before the king's justices – was originally a warning of what
might happen, not the primary purpose of the action. Only as
both tenant and lord began to see advantages in using the
king's court did these assizes become regular means of starting
litigation at the centre. Disseisin did not, in the twelfth
century, imply forcible dispossession by another: Milsom
rightly emphasizes that if this had been so, life at the time
would have been impossibly violent and uncertain, seeing how
often the assize issued. The traditional picture presupposes a
degree of lawlessness not otherwise apparent in the record, as
dispossessors again and again entered upon another's land and
forced him to recover at law what was his own. Rather,
disseisin represents the failure of the lord to bestow seisin
where by the custom of his own court it should go; the
claimant is not trying to recover lands taken from him but asks
that what by binding custom should be his should not be
conferred upon another. His right of seisin is defined in the
relationship between vassal and lord and signified in a piece of
land: that is the way the age thinks of the matter. But if the lord
breaks the rules – for instance, by passing over an heir and
granting seisin to another – the offended party is unlikely to
find a remedy in the local court and seeks an order from the
king, telling the lord to do the right thing. Milsom, of course,
works this out in great detail and for all the so-called
possessory assizes.

In the end, the two pictures differ in emphasis rather than
essentials, but the difference is nonetheless great. As Milsom

sees it, Maitland antedated the settled and sophisticated state of the law by a hundred years at least, whereas in his view the feudal relationships predominated down to the end of the twelfth century over the king's rule, with lords reigning in their lands and the royal courts at most offering *ad hoc* assistance to an aggrieved party against his lord. Out of that assistance grew certainties of possession enforced by the king's courts, but this happy state was not achieved until the powerful realities of the feudal chain of command had been polished away through the increasing interference from above and the work of generations of lawyers who systematized a centralized structure out of the confused and particularized interaction in which what the lords said counted and kings were confined to urging those powerful men to behave by the rules. The difference between Maitland and Milsom may be illustrated by their views concerning the law of inheritance. Maitland regarded it as effectively settled by the middle of the twelfth century: a tenant could use the king's court to compel his lord to grant seisin to a man who claimed by right of his ancestor's seisin. The lord has thus lost all control over who should hold of him once he had made the original grant to a man who came to have heirs. According to Milsom, this was the end product of a long process during which the lord claimed and exercised his right to place seisin where he saw fit, applying accepted rules, but himself deciding what in a given case those rules meant, and making a decision against which there could be no present or future appeal. It was this long process that Maitland drastically foreshortened, thereby giving us quite the wrong view of that earlier and genuinely feudal society. Maitland's splendid quip that the feudal system was introduced into England by Sir Henry Spelman (a seventeenth-century historian) and flourished best in the eighteenth century is a perfectly sound rebuff to those who treat the English kingdom as 'feudal' down to the Tudor age – as many then did, and Marxists still do. But it does overlook the likelihood that it took more than one king, even a Conqueror, to triumph over the social structure and world of ideas within which he had been able to conquer England in the first place.[55]

To sum up: as Milsom says, when Edward I came to the throne 'the world was as Maitland saw it',[56] but he was mistaken in thinking that its notions and commonplaces had remained unchanged for 200 years. Needless to say, we can again find signs that Maitland was not unaware of this: he once admitted that when placing himself in the last quarter of the thirteenth century he was 'dealing with institutions that are already decadent. The feudal scheme of public law has seen its best or worst days.'[57] However, it is really misleading to identify 'the feudal scheme' with any law that can properly be called public (lords' law and king's law were both private and particular to cases as they arose), and also he backdated its decay markedly too far and thus endowed Henry II with an anachronistic attitude to the duties, functions and potential of a king.

I have dwelt at length on what might appear to be a very esoteric dispute because Milsom seems to me to have put his finger on some real weaknesses in Maitland's historical method. No attempt has yet been made to assess this new interpretation, and for all I know Milsom may not in the end prevail: though I must say that he makes excellent sense to one who is a historian without any training in the law. His account incorporates the fact of continuous change in ways that Maitland's fails to do, which means that it fits the experience of the historian but not of the lawyer. Maitland, of course, was a historian too and knew all about change through time, but as we shall see he could unconsciously fall victim at times to his lawyer's training.

Enough has in any case been said to show that Maitland's towering achievement differs from the Bible: his works are not law or revelation. We can be quite sure that of all the people involved he would have been the first to insist on this fact. The thought that he might have brought the history of the law to a standstill by the authority of his writings would have horrified him, and we shall have occasion to point to his influence as the sower of seeds rather than the builder of permanent structures.[58] What he did build, of course, was monumental enough to last a very long time, and his gift for seeing difficulties and weaknesses in his own arguments (another of the true historian's gifts that he possessed) assisted in his monolithic survival. No one more frequently hinted at qualifications and possibilities which, pressed by time, he could not pursue further. Monoliths, excellent objects for worship, are of little use to the study of history. It is therefore important to realize that much work has been done since his time, that the history of England and its law does not now stand where it stood on the day that F. W. Maitland was alive and dead, and that he was quite correct in thinking himself not perfect. What matters next is to identify the sources of his imperfections, such as they were, because understanding them adds further to the lessons which Maitland taught to historians.

Much of the revision done since Maitland's day simply represents the progress of research, commonly under inspirations received from him. New sources are opened up, old ones studied afresh; new theories open vistas, old ones return to make sure that the road leads through real country, not the fantasies of the dogmatizers; all historical understanding grows out of debates and dialectics which ensure that no question can ever be thought of as finally settled, while every question so handled comes by devious routes ever closer to some effective truth. Many of the detailed corrections and revisions applied to Maitland's edifices in the last hundred years are of this mundane and respectable kind. It has also become plain that even he, master as he was of accurate speed, at times worked too fast. He read enormously and remembered tenaciously, and he had an exceptional gift for associating disparate and scattered detail in an all-embracing mind, but no one can see everything. His fundamental error over Bracton owed much to the fact that he had seen only some of the extant manuscripts: since putting this matter right called for several people's labours over seventy years, the shortcoming is no blame to him and worth mentioning only as a warning to those – some still survive – who will not believe that he could ever have failed to know everything relevant to his work. As Maitland kept telling people, the Public Record Office holds mountains of stuff which need to be worked through before anything resembling certainty can be achieved; what remains so impressive are both his awareness of the unexplored ranges and the amount he managed to do with the parts of them that he had himself been able to explore.

This is not, however, the whole story. Why did he stop the history of English law round about 1300? One reason seems to have been his quite genuine desire to get the book done before Pollock could insist on contributing any more to it, a reason which Milsom fairly enough calls bizarre.[59] If one man, even a giant, had to be able to manage that, the timespan needed limiting. There was also the fact, of which he showed himself very well aware, that from the beginning of the fourteenth century the state of the sources alters drastically; with the arrival of the Year Books and the proliferation of plea rolls the writing of legal history assumes a very different dimension, quite unmanageable by one man. Look at the long row of Selden Society volumes – ninety-seven by now and nearly all attendant upon the times that followed the age of Bracton! Much of the history of English law in the later middle ages is written there.

However, Maitland who usually avoided dubious and sweeping statements twice spoke in terms which ring an alarm bell: this should not be ignored. Perhaps the most shocking thing (shocking to the historian) he ever wrote was the explanation of his interest in the land law of Henry III's day: that interest 'will lie in this, that it is capable of becoming the land law of the England, the America, the Australia of the twentieth century'.[60] Quite obviously that was not what drove him to wrestle with seisin, tenure and all the rest: so why did he say it? And in another place he defended as 'sound and truthful' the legal tradition that English law after Edward I had been of an unbroken continuity, so much so that what applied under Edward III was still in effect alive in his own day. He acknowledged that this conviction was 'not all true' but allowed 'it to be in the main . . . truthful'.[61] It is a little ironic that in that very passage Maitland should speak of 'the besetting sin . . . of antedating the emergence of modern ideas', since now it appears that he himself antedated the emergence of old ideas. Even before the destruction of the inherited system in the second half of the nineteenth century, any conviction that little or nothing had changed since 1300 was entirely untrue, but it was what later lawyers salvaged from Sir Edward Coke's faith in an immemorial law and what they preserved by the manner in which they approached their sources and wrote their history. As Milsom says, 'You look on centuries of material generated on the premise that nothing much must be seen to have changed, and write a book saying that nothing much changed.'[62] Maitland usually knew better: he understood the need to look at the past with no thought for its future. But that was not the way lawyers thought, nor the way that most historians of Maitland's day thought who wished to trace 'developments' to their contemporary condition. Maitland, who helped to teach us the error of those ways, stood at the beginning of an era: he worked out principles for others to learn from. No wonder that on occasion he fell victim to the predominant climate surrounding him. Thus, his concentration on the thirteenth century was assisted by a conviction that in that age the law that he knew received its classic formation and the foundations which remained for centuries. That is to say that despite himself he was capable of falling into the teleological error.

The damaging consequences of those rare slips received support from two other facets of his method. We have noted his practice of starting from one central source – from Bracton, from Domesday, from Lyndwood – and we have also had occasion to notice that this practice in part derives from the lawyer's training which accustoms a man to finding a major authority surrounded by commentaries and glosses. Much of Maitland's work answers to that description. The practice works in law because the great lawyer automatically constructs comprehensive answers out of the raw materials so offered, and Milsom, with reason, has pointed out the effect of such proceedings upon Maitland whose exceptional clarity of mind constructed exceptionally coherent and convincing 'pictures' (synthesizing schemes).[63] But the structural principle thus obtained is imposed upon, not extracted from, the confusions of the real world: 'That,' as Milsom puts it, 'is how the law works, and largely how it changes. The change is in the premises from which a matter is approached' – and by himself changing the premises he proceeds to change the picture. However, this is not how history works or changes: the historian may well come to alter the existing picture by questioning its premises, but he should not replace one set of premises by another until he has searched the record with as much freedom from organizing systems as he can manage – the more the very much better. Though Maitland did a great deal of precisely that, at times, in order to present his findings, he had recourse to the lawyer's method, and it could get him into trouble.

Because Maitland knew so much his premises often worked and his pictures withstood the pressure of later research, though how much that endurance owed to the lucidity and concreteness with which they were described is something that only the future will show, now that Maitland is at last ceasing to be the god whose word must never be questioned. It is, however, already apparent that one of his preferred ways of working contributed to the risk of teleological error which like all of us he ran at all times and avoided more commonly than most of us. He believed that dark ages can be illuminated by working backwards from a position upon which light has dawned. This was expressly what he meant to do in *Domesday Book and Beyond*, where 'beyond' means 'before', but he followed much the same precept when he approached the history of the law since the Conquest to 1278 by taking his stand with the outcome and tracking back to the origins. He did marvels with that method, and only the expansion of the archives has rendered it supererogatory in most cases, but it is one with a teleological thread built in. The past must be led up to a known present, and in the journey one encounters very grave dangers that the known present may get unhistorically projected backwards. In addition, such parts of the past as did not make it into the known present are liable to get discarded. Maitland's demonstrable errors – well, for the present highly doubtful expositions – concerning seisin, the role of the crown, the disappearance of seigneurial justice, the prehistory of the established writ system, all owe more than a little to this backward-working technique. Of course, Maitland knew that the historian should work forward without thinking about the outcome, but he rightly thought that there are problems in history where the state of the evidence prohibits such proper methods; he knew his risks but did not always see when he had failed to avoid them. Milsom is probably right in his allegation that even Maitland, who kept emphasizing the fact that unchanging terms keep on changing the contents of their meaning, had difficulties on occasion, when faced with terms like tenure or inheritance, in realizing how much the overtones of the thirteenth century had already changed what those identical words had meant a hundred years earlier.

Lastly, Maitland's sources – virtually all of them products of the king's government – together with some convictions and preoccupations of his own day could induce him to overestimate the power, initiative and ingenuity of the realm's central bodies – to predate centralized kingship and unifying principles. Centralized kingship and unifying principles form one of the main threads of English law and English history: no wonder that this lawyer–historian was perhaps a little too ready to see them at work a little too early or too successfully. I speak as a non-lawyer historian who in his time has been overimpressed by the work of a centralizing monarchy. It is, I think, becoming clear that neither Henry II nor his agents were so consciously engaged in providing a royal law in supersession of diversified customs as Maitland tended to suppose. Of course, once again he was the first to express doubts. Writing to an American colleague in 1889, he could not help thinking 'that the law of the King's courts is only a part of the law, and that the lawyers in those courts, having to do only with the remedies there given, get into a way of speaking about "property" which really is misleading'.[64] It could be charged that when the *History of English Law* came out six years later too little of this true insight appeared in it.

Criticizing Maitland is a dangerous game: so often one finds that he has been there first, and he wrote so much that it is far too easy to miss something. No wonder that the worshippers have had their own way for so long. Yet it is necessary to point out that even he could err quite dramatically at times because his method, the source of such learned success, had its weaknesses. In his day few people analysed even their own historical methods beyond such obvious needs as the study of original documents properly understood, the elimination of forgeries, correct dating of the undated. Maitland, it would seem instinctively (being that sort of scholar), did most things right and always remained uncertain about much that he wrote about: he knew that the search for total knowledge, total certainty, meant only total silence. The intermediate answer is what needs to be offered, and he did not expect his intermediate answers to sit unchallenged for so long. Nevertheless, reliance on a single source with the rest gathered predictably around it, together with a predilection for a clarity far beyond the powers of those who in the circumstances of their own day made the law of which he spoke, could at times produce errors not explicable solely by an inevitable inability to read everything or singlehandedly in a brief lifetime to do the work of dozens in a century. Even Maitland erred – and only of Maitland among all English historians through the ages is it even necessary to record the fact.

Generalizations are all very well, but if we are really to understand Maitland's stature as a historian and his long hold on other historians' affectionate awe we need to look more closely at him as he worked. We will therefore turn to four particular case studies, all of them outside his central labours on the common law of the thirteenth century. They are chosen, as I will freely admit, because their themes fall more within my area of competence than does that law, but also because, being more limited and concentrated, they offer a better chance to bring Maitland alive.

3 Four Cases

The Early Parliament

In January 1889, the deputy keeper of the public records, Henry Maxwell Lyte, took yet another initiative when he invited the Downing professor to investigate and edit the unsorted bundles of petitions presented in Edward I's Parliaments. Maxwell Lyte, anxious to get at least the medieval records in his keeping put into usable order, initiated the policy of using the services of editors not on his staff which was and remains exiguous. (The policy continues to be pursued.) Maitland declared himself interested, but a study of the materials in question quickly persuaded him that the original proposal demanded more than any man could manage. By June he knew that as a first step one would have to date the normally undated petitions and that even a diligent man could not hope to despatch more than a thousand in a year, working continuously. He himself, he said, could not spare more than two months in the year for work at the Office. When further study persuaded him that he could after all trust the modern dates put upon the documents by earlier editors who (in the criminal manner then common) appeared to have broken up dated files, he resumed work, but was soon stopped by an experience familiar to habitués of the Record Office: essential materials could not be produced because they were 'under arrangement'. Meanwhile, however, he had come across a hitherto unpublished roll of Parliament which had lain hidden until the transfer of the archives to Chancery Lane had revealed its existence, and in October he therefore proposed a new idea to the deputy keeper. He would edit this roll, for the Lenten Parliament of 1305, by tracking and printing the original petitions upon which its entries rested, as well as the evidence (on charter, patent and close rolls) of action taken as a result of decisions made in the Parliament. This, he suggested, would provide a first step towards the proper calendaring of the petitions by showing what could be done. Lyte accepted the proposal for the officially sponsored Rolls Series, long ailing and soon to expire. The result of eight months' deliberations was the volume generally known by its half-title as Maitland's *Memoranda de Parliamento*, put into the world with Maitland's usual speed in 1893.[1] This book, disparagingly described as hackwork by one of Maitland's admirers,[2] turned out to be Maitland's most explosive contribution to English history.

When Maitland tackled the Parliament roll of 1305 – really an artificial entity made up of pieces found in the medley of loose Exchequer documents – the orthodox view of the early Parliament of England had been firmly laid down by Stubbs; and though Stubbs expressed himself with some care and with words of caution, it derived directly from the interpretations offered by the antiquaries of the sixteenth and seventeenth centuries. According to this view (to give a brief and perhaps too concise account) the Parliament was from the first an assembly of the estates, representing the various orders of which English society was composed (clergy, nobility and commons), called by the king to discuss and advise on the great affairs of the nation, to validate his legislative edicts, and to authorize his collection of taxes. The Parliament of 1295, which did contain all those estates, was dubbed the 'Model Parliament', and though, of course, further developments – more particularly the disappearance of the lower clergy and the emergence of two Houses in place of the three estates – were recognized, the accepted version held that from 1295 at the latest the Parliament of England was a political body, the representative element in a constitution in which the king governed by consent. The fact that the first formal calling of the Commons (1258) had been the work of Simon de Montfort during a power struggle with the crown, and the accident of Edward II's reign when the king mostly stood at odds with an aristocracy who used the Parliament against him and needed allies among the knights and burgesses, confirmed this established view. Except for details in composition, length and frequency of meetings, and the distribution of power within it, the medieval Parliament from Edward I onwards was seen as identical with the Parliaments of the seventeenth and nineteenth centuries – the nation in session, and charged with the task of counterbalancing the power of royal government.

Stubbs recognized some of the difficulties raised by this vision. Thus the notion of a political body participating in rule marched awkwardly with the three annual Parliaments prescribed by the Provisions of Oxford of 1258 as well as with the demands for very frequent Parliaments recurring down to the fifteenth century. Were there really enough 'great affairs' afoot to occupy such meetings, and how did members feel about the constant coming and going that would have been involved? The well-attested reluctance of representatives to turn up at all stood in conflict with their supposed role. But such things could, with a little effort, be accommodated to the image of a Parliament which stood over against the king and controlled his exercise of power. The history of the institution was in fact greatly influenced by the accident that the parties of the seventeenth-century civil war were traditionally called king and Parliament. Obviously, these two entities must have been in conflict, potential or real, at all times, and obviously the relations with each other culminating in the ultimate triumph of the second over the first provided the main thread of English history.

There is no sign that Maitland doubted this description before he came to work on the roll of 1305. In his lectures, written in 1887–8, he adduces much detail that should have made him wonder whether the history of Parliament was really the history of national politics, but he fully accepted the misconceived teaching on the three estates and their function in government, though he knew that even by 1307 the powers of the king acting with his Council had not 'been transferred to an assembly of estates'. That transfer, however, was the destiny of the English constitution, and the assembly of 1295 'gives us the model for all future parliaments'.[3] He spent a lot of time talking about the estates, seemingly without realizing that only fiction – the fiction of the middle ages settled in the seventeenth century – had ever introduced them into the story of English government. In essentials, in 1888 his Parliament is the Parliament of Stubbs. Then he looked at the records of the 1305 Parliament, a Parliament which appeared to follow the 'model', and he found himself compelled to conclude that what he saw there differed strangely and strikingly from the inherited stereotype.

If what assembled at Westminster in the Lent of 1305 were 'the estates' there was no sign at all that any of them acted as cohesive and distinguishable groups; in his references to what he had caused to be gathered there the king did not speak of estates but of particular people by ranks – archbishops, bishops, other prelates (that is, abbots), earls, barons, knights and burgesses (where were the proctors of the lower clergy? – a point which Maitland passed over). The full assembly sat for three weeks, after which everybody but the members of the king's Council (prelatical, noble, judges 'and others') were sent home, with a warning that if needed they would have to come back. This indication that their despatch did not terminate the Parliament was indeed borne out by events: for nearly three more weeks the conciliar remnant continued to sit and continued to be called 'un plein parlement'. There has been much debate whether 'plein' meant open or full, but those are futile arguments: what matters is that the truncated body, reduced to the king and his Council, continued to be regarded as quite as much the Parliament as the larger assembly of the earlier weeks had been. The work carried out by this body (in full session or by means of committees), before and after the reduction, turned out to be even more surprising. Although the writ of summons had spoken of 'certain matters specially touching our realm of England and the establishment

59

of our land of Scotland', if any such great affairs were debated they left no trace in the record: Maitland felt forced to conclude that the evidence did not permit him to suppose that the king wished to discuss them with the 'estates'. There was no proper legislation: no statute was promulgated, and though certain decisions in response to petitions achieved the character of more general ordinances, they were made by the king and his Council, with no reference to assent or even advice from the other persons there. The king asked for no money; the only mention of taxing occurred in petitions from lesser lords and abbeys, seeking the king's agreement to their mulcting their own tenants.

In fact, the vast bulk of the business of the meeting, both before and after the departure of the estates, consisted in the settlement of the affairs of private men, as the king considered and answered their petitions. Some of that activity could be called judicial, the settling of legal disputes, but Maitland could see no clear line between this and the granting of other kinds of petition (for favour and such like). He spent much time in analysing the king's Council, incidentally eliminating the various adjectival forms – great, general, privy and so forth – which doctrine had invented and the record knew nothing of;[4] and he concluded that in effect this so-called Parliament (and it called itself a Parliament) was the king's government in fullest session, dealing with the affairs of both king and subject. So he had to maintain that it was not the estates that formed the core of the Parliament but this function belonged to the Council – a genuine institution incorporating all the king's professional officers and all his courts. The Parliament itself was 'rather an act than a body of persons'.[5] With the precision that can come to the historian who actually reads his sources he identified Parliament as an emergent court, more intermittent, of course, than those *coram rege* (King's Bench) and *de banco* (Common Pleas) but distinguishable as a separate court because it produced a formal plea roll of its own which we call the Parliament roll. He drew attention to the definition found in the virtually contemporary treatise called

Fleta whose author, having spoken of the king's various courts, goes on to explain that furthermore 'the king holds his court in his Council in Parliaments, in the presence of prelates, earls, barons, nobles and other learned men', which court determines dubious points of law and creates new remedies for new wrongs. That is to say, Parliament appeared to be what its long-lasting title indicated – a session of the high court of the realm and the occasion for the dispensing of justice that could not be dealt with elsewhere.

Maitland's Parliament now differed fundamentally from Stubbs's. It was part of the king's government, one of his agencies of administration, intermittent because such plenary sessions of all his ministers and judges neither could nor needed to be called all that frequently. It was a session of the king with his Council (and before long, we may add, that Council was to include not only the permanent professional body but also the so-called councillors born, the later House of Lords) who met people sent up from the localities to receive instructions, testify to cooperation, and bring up the problems of the kingdom in one convenient place for the king to settle with the advice of his Council. This was no assembly of estates representing the political power of the nation, but the nation coming summoned as suitors to the king's highest court. Its conceptual ancestry lies not in any Roman *comitia* but in the right of any lord to impose suit of court upon his vassals.

The revolutionary implications of this drastic revision of what had become the central theme of English constitutional history took a long time to make themselves felt. Few people read introductions to the editions of obscure medieval documents; they read compendia and general histories. In addition, Maitland, in his usual manner, confined himself to gentle hints and avowed, contrary to the truth, that his findings did not depart 'very far from the path marked out by books that are already classical'.[6] He had in mind the tradition enshrined in Stubbs which he had just overthrown in five thumping propositions:

61

1. A session of the king's Council is 'the core and essence of every *parliamentum*'.
2. The so-called 'parliamentary petitions' are petitions to the king and his Council.
3. The auditors of petitions are not 'the parliament' but committees of the Council.
4. 'The rolls of parliament are the record of the business done by the council, – sometimes with, but much more often without, the concurrence of the estates of the realm.'
5. The highest tribunal in England is not a general assembly of barons and prelates but the king's Council.

Not one of these propositions fitted the received opinion; between them, they marked a totally new start on the history of Parliament.

In due course the slow-fused bomb exploded. In 1910, the American scholar Charles McIlwain published a book built on the premise that Parliament was, above all else, a court for the dispensing of justice, though by extending the medieval truths into the seventeenth century he obscured developments and created new error.[7] McIlwain acknowledged his debt to the *Memoranda* in his introduction; in another place he called Maitland 'the greatest modern master'.[8] As tended to happen to people who took up suggestions put forward by this master, McIlwain overbalanced the argument on the other side: Maitland had never said that Parliament was *only* a high court. Moreover, McIlwain was more interested in political and legal ideas than in political action, and the first full exploitation of Maitland's revolution fell to the Tudor historian A. F. Pollard, who lacked not only Maitland's subtlety but also his modesty.[9] His enterprise was brave: he wished to write a general essay on the history of Parliament, starting from Maitland but tracing the great 'evolutionary' changes that had in the end produced the modern institution. A good Gladstonian liberal, he treated Parliament with a kind of dour adoration and a massive as well as repulsive insularity. Representative institutions, the culmination of man's political developments, everywhere, he said, owed everything to the English model: all such bodies, whatever their names, really derived from the example of Westminster. If the transplant had not taken everywhere the fault lay with the recipients: 'the failure of parliamentary institutions in semitic or negroid communities is proof, not of the defects of parliaments but of the political incapacity of those who cannot work them.'[10] Add to this a reasonable ignorance of the middle ages, a failure to use manuscript materials, an unhappy capacity for supporting his more daring statements with footnotes that seem to have nothing to say about the matter at issue, and it is not surprising that Pollard came near to killing off the influence of Maitland which he generously acknowledged.[11]

However, before medievalists' furious reaction to this rash intruder could bury Maitland in the same grave as his ill-advised disciple the problems of parliamentary history were taken up by H. G. Richardson and G. O. Sayles, who from the mid–1920s poured forth editions, articles and books on both the English and the Irish Parliaments that took up Maitland's torch and built a whole new interpretation around it. Sayles has lately produced a short book drawing together the results of this life's work by a formidable and uncompromising pair of scholars, and this book makes it easy to see what they have done.[12] Their real concern lay with the early Parliaments, before the accession of Edward II, and the essential article of faith was stated by Sayles some thirty-five years ago: 'The vital force in parliament was the council with all its subordinate committees and tribunals.' Thus Maitland's innovation became doctrine. Sayles rightly went on to ask the question 'why parliament became separated into kings, lords and commons, and concentrated on politics rather than the dispensation of justice', a development which he believed had happened by the later fourteenth century.[13] I do not think that it had: politics in any real sense remained marginal to Parliaments, while from its role as a justice-dispensing court grew its role as legislator. However, the late-medieval Parliament has not had its Richardson and Sayles and awaits real study; meanwhile one of Sayles's insights is worth quoting because it too comes straight out of Maitland: the changing Parliament, he affirmed, 'was no different from its predecessors in being an expression of the royal prerogative and not of any "national will".'[14]

However, traditions do not lie down that easily, least of all traditions warranted by Stubbs.[15] The liberal mind revolted against a Parliament which was the king's instrument and possession, a Parliament which could exist without the Commons and played a political role if aristocratic hostility to the crown found there a stage on which to conduct its conflicts. The most violent reaction, rather surprisingly, came from Bertie Wilkinson, normally a peaceful man. He categorically denied that Parliament ever equalled the king's Council or was a mere expansion of it, and he attacked not only Pollard but the heresiarch himself.[16] Convinced that from the first a true Parliament was one in which the common interests of the realm were discussed – that is, political issues – and convinced that it was 'the greatest of all expressions of the medieval tradition of government by consent', Wilkinson even had the nerve to question Maitland's translations from the medieval French at crucial points. He overreached himself and defeated the cause he was trying to serve. Peace was gradually restored by other historians, particularly Sir Goronwy Edwards, who rather out-Maitlanded Maitland while professing to reintroduce Stubbs: if Parliaments, he pointed out, were sessions of the whole government of England then all sorts of matters were obviously and properly discussed there. Eminently judicious rather than doctrinaire, as always, he allowed the principle of consent to have played its part, but derived it from administrative convenience rather than from principle.[17] Anodyne but reasonably convincing, with the Maitland yeast worked so well into the Stubbs flour that it has ceased to bubble. Edwards succeeded in carrying Maitland's developing Parliament beyond the point where Sayles leaves it. At present it looks as though agreement may have been reached at least on the early Parliaments, but one may doubt whether the full effects of *Memoranda de Parliamento* have yet been worked out even for the middle ages. A non-medievalist had better leave it there.

On the other hand, a non-medievalist is entitled to affirm that these effects have still to make themselves felt in the history of Parliament after 1485 and more particularly from the seventeenth century onwards. This is in the main because thoughts of political conflict still dominate the minds of too many historians, but there is also the problem that after about 1500 the institution underwent a transformation which, while at first sight contrary to the Maitland 'model', in fact operates inside it: Parliament remains the king's instrument of government but inner structure and major concerns alter. In the sixteenth century the medieval high court spectacularly became a sovereign legislative assembly by including the king together with the two Houses in what Henry VIII once called 'one body politic',[18] and by the last decade it had moved a long way towards becoming the arena of national politics. Yet until 1693 its existence remained dependent on the king's will, and thereafter too the king, or the government that came to exercise his powers, just about always remained firmly in control of it. When Maitland spoke of the king and his Council as the core and essence of the Parliament of Edward I he was making no claims for the subsequent 600 years and more, and I have no reason to think that he would have endorsed a view which saw the fundamental truth of that description still operate in his own day. Yet it is my conviction that all historians concerned to understand Parliament throughout its existence would be well advised to heed the lead he gave us.

The English Parliament started, as Maitland showed, as an instrument of royal government, and it has always remained just that. Since one of its functions has been to enable the king and his agents to govern more effectively by giving them a chance to discover in time how actions of government might be received by the governed, there have always been opportunities for debate, dispute, criticism and even conflict.

These have been misread into strange notions of kings calling Parliaments which were designed to hamper their actions by opposing them. Parliament, of course, was and remains meant to provide a better way of exercising rule, not shackles on rulership. That is why Edward I called it; that is why Henry VIII called it; that is what to this day it does for the party in power. Until very recently it did not even inhibit secret government when ministers wished to govern secretly. It will come as a shock to the self-important people who fill opposition back-benches, but theirs is a largely decorative role because that of the whole Parliament is, as it were, subsidiary: governing with and through it makes the work easier because – and that was the discovery of the thirteenth century – you get better results when you seem to be able to claim consent for your decisions. Of course, this limits arbitrary rule by an individual, which is a good thing. Does it, however, limit arbitrary rule by a clique, of whatever persuasion? The learned, technical and penetrating introduction to the edition of one old roll has after ninety years still not lost its power to make us look more closely and more clearly at what politicians ignorant of history and historians untutored in politics have made into an idealized and over-valued institution in the realm.

By way of a footnote I should like to add a point which, though Maitland rather unaccountably missed it, gives further support to his analysis. He asked why cases came before the king in his Parliament rather than before some other tribunal, a question to which, he thinks, we often cannot give 'a certain answer'. He concludes that the decisive criterion must have been the importance of the causes – 'important because they concern the king, or because they concern very great men, or because they involve grave questions of public law, or because they are unprecedented'.[19] However, the cases on his roll do not by any means all fit into one of these categories. Here Maitland allowed a preoccupation with settled institutions to direct his thought, a preoccupation which is inappropriate to the scene. What he overlooked is the pressure of suitors for justice – or advantage.

Suitors will always go as high as they can in order to get the most authoritative and least appealable resolution for their needs and ambitions. In a system which emphasizes the residue of judicial power in the crown after regular tribunals for specific cases have been set up – and in effect this system, varying much in detail, lasted till the eighteenth century – the search on the part of the subject for a way to by-pass the usual channels and get a quick decision in answer to a petition remained one of the constants of public life. So, in consequence, did the efforts made by these last-in-the-line agencies to reduce the flood of petitions reaching them. In 1305, as Maitland himself showed, a first sorting of petitions transferred a good many to existing courts, but especially because Scotland and Gascony also came to seek justice at Westminster this preliminary work still left a vast burden of mixed matters to be settled by the Council in Parliament. If the king found Parliament useful because it enabled him to govern the realm from one place, so did his subjects welcome the opportunity to bring their problems to the seat of government. These matters are the 'grievances' of Tudor and Stuart Parliaments – not by any means necessarily complaints of tyranny or misgovernment but much more commonly unsettled titles in land, insufficient protection for manufacturers, unfair rules in the law, the need for a bridge here or defences against the sea there. Under Edward I petitions produced royal answers; under the Tudors (who possessed other instruments for dealing with the strictly private disputes and requests that came before the Parliament of 1305) the bills that had descended from those earlier petitions produced, if they were lucky, acts of Parliament.

As constant as the flood of petitions are the devices for rendering the quantity manageable. As early as 1279, the Chancery recorded a royal memorandum to the effect that the petitions that made the time of Parliament burdensome to king and Council should be reduced by sending the main part to other courts, leaving the Parliament only with matters that could not be settled elsewhere.[20] The Council hoped in vain: this note runs through centuries of the history of English government. In the course of the fourteenth century petitions in Parliament did get reduced to those that could be seen as worthy of forming the basis of the limited number of decrees issued there: we are on our way to a legislative rather than a judicial treatment of those 'grievances'. But this proved possible only because the Council managed to unload the bulk of petitions onto the chancellor, who in this way came to preside over the settled court of Chancery in the course of the fifteenth century. By about 1500 the chancellor's jurisdiction had become sufficiently defined for him to be unable to deal with many matters raised by petition: hence the new courts of Star Chamber and Requests as specialized aspects of Council activity and supposed relievers of the Council as a true governing body. It worked after a fashion but by no means the way it had been intended: suitors knew well enough that if they could get at the Privy Council directly they could even outflank that same Council sitting as the court of Star Chamber. The Elizabethan Privy Council time and again, and always in vain, tried to stop litigants from crowding its agenda. Then a kind of historical irony asserted itself: early in James I's reign, Robert Cecil thought that he might find the answer to the problem in Parliament and tried to get Commons committees to hear petitions transferred from the Council Board. This never worked, but by 1621, by an even more pointed irony, the Upper House began to take on the job. The regular jurisdiction of the House of Lords, active in the 1640s and settled in the reign of Charles II, really took its origin from its willingness to hear and adjudicate litigants' complaints. This did not stop a continued increase in the number of private petitions addressed to the Parliament, handling which became in the eighteenth century the busiest activity of the Lords sitting ostensibly not as a court but as a House; the actual work was done by a few men, usually the chairman of committees assisted by the judges.[21] Only in the nineteenth century did the crown finally lock away its residual power to do justice; since then only legislation, or ministerial order under an act, have been able to create new machinery and new remedies.

Behind the House of Lords acting as a court stood the pressure of petitions that at one time had forced the king's Council to hold judicial sessions in Parliament. The history of Parliament, which in one respect is contained in the king's need to govern more efficiently, in another is enclosed in that circular progression as the king's subjects searched for what they called justice. Maitland firmly delineated what kings and ministers wanted from Parliament, but he only just hinted what other parts of the nation wanted from kings and ministers in Parliament. Both sides found the occasions of parliamentary meetings actually or potentially very useful: no wonder that Parliament took root. This is not the whole story and politics are not to be forgotten, but it is, as Maitland taught us, the hard centre of the story.

Canon Law

In the summer of 1895, Maitland was assailed by spiritual doubt. He was engaged in writing some lectures on the history of the canon law and encountered a strongly entrenched opinion which seemed to him to be contradicted by the sources. Unsure of the degree of his heterodoxy he consulted Reginald Lane Poole, editor of the *English Historical Review*, who evidently encouraged him to go on. Within the year, Maitland's first essay on the subject appeared in that journal (in those days even journal editors moved at speed); two more followed it. In 1898, Maitland collected the three papers, added three earlier ones concerned with matters of the Church's law, and published the whole collection as *Roman Canon Law in the Church of England*. At the last he briefly hesitated when he heard that Bishop Stubbs felt 'sore' at being criticized, but fortunately he went on. As he told Fisher in 1905, he had 'got more fun out of that than out of

any job I ever did'. The fun came in the pompous ex-
postulations that the book brought him from outraged
clergy, the latest being a missive 'from one Walsh'. This,
though he did not know it, was William Walsh, Roman
Catholic archbishop of Dublin, whose proper description he
could not gather from the letter. Stranded in his winter exile
without a copy of *Who's Who*, he risked 'eminence'; Mrs
Maitland had suggested 'holy sir'.[22]

The matter at issue was this. In 1883, a Royal Commission
investigating the ecclesiastical courts, of which Commission
Stubbs was a member, issued a report in which it declared,
among many other things, that 'the canon law of Rome,
though always regarded as of great authority in England, was
not held to be binding on the courts' in the middle ages. This
conclusion was supported by Stubbs in a long 'Historical
Appendix'. Behind these apparently harmless words lay a
turmoil of present politics, namely the Anglo-Catholic movement and the growing threat of a massive secession from the
Church of England to Rome. These enemies within held that at
the Reformation the English Church had clearly separated
itself from the Universal Church and that therefore it was no
Apostolic Church. Against this attack, stalwart Anglicans,
also menaced on the other side by the well-established
Methodist schism which had added large numbers to the body
of Nonconformists, wished to believe that the Church of
England had always been an entity of its own, only loosely
linked to the papacy at Rome even before the Reformation. If
it could claim that the law of its medieval courts stood on its
own feet, respecting the law emanating from Rome but not
bound to obey unless it expressly chose to do so, its continuity
across the alleged chasm of the sixteenth century would
receive historical endorsement. That is what Stubbs, summing
up widely held views, wished to supply.

And this view Maitland found it impossible to reconcile
with his reading of the sources: he attacked it with wit and
abandon. Relying mainly on the *Provinciale* (1430) of William
Lyndwood, archiepiscopal judge of Canterbury, but using also

other canonistic writings, he worked out the opinion of England's leading experts concerning the law to be used in the Church courts. He left no doubt at all that to those canonists the papal edicts constituted the source of binding law; such provinces of the Universal Church as Canterbury and York could legislate at best by what Maitland called 'bye-laws' – local edicts which could only clarify or elaborate in detail where Rome had laid down general rules. 'Whereas,' he declared, 'the English state was an independent whole, the English church was in the eyes of its own judges a dependent fragment whose laws had been imposed on it from without.'[23] Where Stubbs's party wished to believe that the Roman canon law applied in England only if it had been expressly received and admitted, Maitland showed that no such choice existed; talk of laws requiring the sanction of established usage meant only that some laws could get obsolete enough to cease to be applicable.[24] Nor could the claim to independence be saved by the fact that some papal constitutions remained a dead letter in England. All that this proves is negligence, sometimes the negligence of self-interest, on the part of the enforcing bishops.[25]

In the second essay Maitland cleared up an extraordinary confusion in part accepted and in part created by Stubbs. The question being whether the Church courts of England felt bound to obey the law coming from Rome, it mattered not at all whether the king's courts in England accepted that law. Thus Stubbs had used the famous reply of the barons at Merton in 1236 – 'we will not have the laws of England altered' – to support his case for independence. That reply concerned a difference between two systems of law touching persons born out of wedlock: the canon law held that their parents' subsequent marriage made them legitimate, the law of England left them bastards all their lives. The barons' refusal endorsed a victory for the common law, no more; as Maitland showed, the bishops on that occasion had refused to answer a question from the judges concerning somebody's legitimacy because they knew that the law they took from Rome did not prevail in the secular courts.[26] Maitland briefly traced some occasions of conflict between the two laws. In the first place, as he demonstrated, while the two sides agreed on their respective regions of competence, there existed a grey area between them where both sides liked to enter claims. Secondly, and arising from those disputable matters, the crown consistently endeavoured to restrict ecclesiastical, especially papal, interference in matters touching the rights of the king, many of which were in fact 'grey'. There was therefore much disputing between the king and the Church, but none between the Church and Rome. Maitland held that in these conflicts the king increasingly got the upper hand, more particularly because from the early fourteenth century onwards the papacy's power declined drastically, not to be revived until the middle of the fifteenth, but that none of this altered the law of the Church courts: it merely limited their ability to make themselves felt. As for the erroneous allegation that the spiritual courts obeyed and even enforced the secular law, he pointed out that the evidence all came from after the Reformation. Whereas the adversary wished, if possible, to eliminate the Reformation altogether or at least treat it as a small and predictable shudder in a general march of continuity, Maitland emphasized that it was a revolution.[27] As he once said in another context, he was dealing with people who wished to believe that the Church of England was Protestant before the Reformation and Catholic after it.

The third essay further hammered down the coffin lid on the false doctrine by demonstrating that William of Drogheda, a leading English (or Irish – no matter here) canonist of the early fourteenth century, totally accepted the 'Hildebrandine' view of the Church according to which it was a single empire ruled by the pope and not a federation of practically independent local Churches. The remaining three essays, of an earlier vintage, treated of particular cases in which secular and spiritual law had interacted in medieval England; important enough in themselves, they were not concerned with the main dispute and caused no disagreements.

For, of course, this devastating attack on a cherished belief, thought necessary for the legitimation of the nineteenth-century Church of England, did not go unnoticed.[28] His revolutionary teaching on Parliament Maitland had inconveniently buried in a little-read edition, but his heterodoxy on the medieval canon law he had not only maintained in the relative obscurity of a learned journal (where Stubbs saw it and grew 'sore') – he put it out in the only one of his mature books not published by his University Press. He meant it to be read, and he enjoyed the rumpus he had caused. How pure were his intentions in this case? In the preface to the book he tried to forestall charges of partisanship by declaring himself unconcerned whether he was thought to be bringing aid to Rome or comfort to Canterbury: 'I am a dissenter from both, and from other churches.' He told Sidgwick that he hoped to escape in peace because both the warring parties had reason for shying away from tackling the problems of the medieval canon law: Anglicans would find it too 'full of ugly holes' to suit their search for continuous independence, while the Romans would dislike discoveries that did not agree with the current orthodoxies (he had the issue of infallibility in mind for which the old law supplied insufficient support). So 'to express a tolerant contempt for lawyers will be the popular and the safe course'.[29] As a matter of fact, the tone of these remarks barely hides a tolerant contempt for clerics. The delight and bubbling irony which spring from the pages of the book did not come from nowhere: at the task of lambasting pretentious prelates and presumptuous priests Maitland ever went with a degree of mild malice that is not to be found elsewhere in his writings. When all has been said, and true as his disavowal of any religious allegiance unquestionably was, Maitland belonged to that not unfamiliar brand of historian who, brought up as a Protestant, retains for the rest of his agnostic days a sympathy for the Reformation as the punishment of clerical arrogance.

Maitland enjoyed himself in proving the medieval Church of England deplorably papalist, but was he right? As one reads these sparkling essays one begins to feel doubts stir. The range of problems covered in some 130 pages is so great, and yet the illustrative examples of cases produced are so few. Once again we find Maitland solving really major questions by working outwards from a single main source, in this case a medieval textbook; can we accept Lyndwood as typical? As Maitland says himself: 'We must not judge a school by a single book, even though it be almost the only book the school produces, and we must not judge a long age by one critical moment.'[30] As always, he goes on to crystallize those very doubts the reader had begun to feel – and quite coolly lays most of them at rest. Still, the range of sources – virtually only commentaries – remains circumscribed, especially when one compares it with what Maitland used in his work on the common law. As we have come to expect, he himself drew attention to that risk when at the end of three devastating essays he remarked that a true history of the medieval Church courts was not yet possible because the actual records of the courts were so far inaccessible.[31] 'They are voluminous,' as indeed they are. They have since been studied at least in part, for Maitland as usual pointed the way, though it was not until 1967 that an act book of a consistory court was at last edited.[32] Surely all that massive work since Maitland's day, using a vastly greater range of sources than he employed, must have made a difference, the more so because Maitland put a case which many of his readers would have been delighted to see refuted. Anglo-Catholicism no longer rides high among bishops or historians, but many a faithless medievalist has inherited the desire to write the Reformation out of English history.

The immediate reaction to *Roman Canon Law in the Church of England* was one of stunned amazement; even Stubbs, no longer active as a historian, slightly amended some things he had said when a new edition of his published lectures came out. A more notably hostile response came from Malcolm MacColl, Anglican canon of Ripon, who thought of himself as a learned defender of the other view; Maitland disposed of him with a courtesy which allowed him only at moments to hint at the exasperation felt by one who at least had 'wetted the soles of my feet on the shore of the medieval *oceanus iuris*' at the effrontery of this numbskull.[33] MacColl had challenged the champion during his life; Arthur Ogle (another high-church cleric whom I had the pleasure still to meet in the 1950s when he had ceased to be high-church and had conceived a dislike for Thomas More) wisely waited till Maitland had died. Even so he proved only the unwisdom of attacking so well armoured a man with a wooden sword.[34] For about a half-century Maitland's views remained unquestioned orthodoxy, repeated, usually without his careful warning about the need for more work, in monographs and textbooks alike. In 1963, Charles Duggan showed that the prevalence in the canon-law *Decretals* of papal decisions touching England did not prove an exceptional English dependence on Rome;[35] but then Maitland had made no such claim, and the critique was better addressed to some who had taken him further than he had gone. Jack Gray thought that Maitland had failed to allow for two signs of independence: English bishops regularly failed to enforce some papal law and frequently failed to press papal complaints before the king.[36] But Maitland had asked whether the English Church could really choose to observe papal law or not; neither negligence (on which in fact he had remarked) nor apprehension of the royal wrath, though they may well indicate a degree of independence from Rome in practice, affect that issue. In 1957, Eric Kemp, himself a canonist, took exception to Maitland's description of the basic texts of the canon law as 'absolutely binding statute law'; he pointed out that a large part of those books consists of specific cases decided at Rome and poorly answers to the title statutes. But Maitland had shown that both the medieval canonists and the English Church courts had treated such case-law as binding, that is as law decreed, so that worrying about the word 'statute' is rather pointlessly pernickety.[37] It is really astonishing how well Maitland's book stood up through decades of quite intensive efforts to assail him on a front which he himself regarded as less well defended than it should have been.

Then, in 1974, a more comprehensive attack was mounted by Charles Donahue.[38] The reader must remember that his long article appeared in a law journal, a fact which explains the air of patiently explaining matters of history to bright infants with which it starts. But once it gets going it opens important questions. Admittedly Donahue sees the purpose of his enquiry in a rather strange light. As a legal historian (he says) he is not much concerned with the relationship between England and Rome. Rather he wants to discover whether it is possible for two legal systems to operate within one country – as though he had never heard of law and equity, two different systems that have coexisted for at least 400 years and on top of that were always operated by the same kind of lawyers. Secondly he wants to find out what 'binding' meant in practice: does a judge 'use law to decide a case' and more specifically, 'how were the papal law books used in the English courts Christian'?[39] The second is a valid question, but as it turns out not well answerable because we too rarely hear what was argued in court.

Half his discussion deals with the relations between the ecclesiastical and the king's courts, the theme of Maitland's second chapter, and would seem to agree with Maitland's conclusion that the common law's objections to the canon law arose from the latter's dependence on the pope rather than the king. Donahue expresses astonishment at the amount of litigation that could have gone to the common law but instead sought out the Church courts: an interesting point though not strengthened by his reliance on clerical jurisdiction over what appear to be contracts. As the book he refers to shows, the Church courts got a footing here through their legitimate jurisdiction over perjury;[40] as he fails to tell us, the deficiencies of the action of covenant left the medieval common law very weak on concerns vital to all sorts of people. He also argues that prohibitions, which stopped an ecclesiastical court from proceeding in a case, were far rarer and less effective than used to be supposed; what he really shows here is that they were, of course, activated only at the request of a party and therefore somewhat unpredictable in incidence.[41] Donahue is right to emphasize that the Church courts stood up better to the assaults of the common law than Maitland supposed, and that they thus retained real importance well into the later sixteenth century at least.[42] However, like Maitland he makes the mistake of treating the apparent struggle between two systems of jurisdiction as an active battle between the king (and his representatives) and the pope (and his dependents). Maitland thought that the crown always won, at least from the later fourteenth century onwards; Donahue points out that weapons available on the crown's side were left to rust and infers an innate strength in the canon law. I suggest that the correct way to see this issue is different from either. Here were two different systems offering remedies in disputes; which was chosen could be up to the litigant or his lawyer; much that was available was thus not used. But even Donahue agrees that when it came to a genuine clash, the courts Christian at best could preserve their dignity while retreating.

Donahue's careful discussion of the relationship between the York diocesan court and the court of Rome puts on the bones of Maitland's argument the kind of flesh that creates the diversity of natural bodies. In effect Donahue shows that papal law operated if available and applicable, but that frequently it needed either supplementing or extending by reliance on local custom – Maitland's 'bye-laws'. To quote:[43]

> If we frame the question of the authority of the canon law in the English church in the terms in which Stubbs and Maitland chose to frame it, then Maitland was right; the papal law was binding. If, however, we regard 'law', not as a series of general propositions to which judges give assent, but rather as a set of rules by which they resolve actual cases, then Stubbs and Maitland were asking the wrong question. The question is not 'Was papal law binding?' It is, in a great many cases, 'Was it law?'

But that is not what he proves, for he shows that indeed it was law – the law by which cases were decided – if it referred, and that for the practical needs of the courts it did not always suffice.

Donahue's chief contribution on the actuality of trials lies in his emphasis on the quantity of cases that never came to judgment. Failure to pursue a cause after starting it was very common, and many a dispute was settled by compromises out of court. This was the common experience of all medieval jurisdictions – systems in which far more depended on the initiatives of the litigants than on the initiatives of courts, and in which litigation was often started not to seek judgment but in order to induce the opponent to come to terms. Maitland read writers of textbooks concerned to give instructions for cases that lasted the course – to tell, that is, both judges and litigants what would happen once the case had commenced, on the supposition that it would go on to the bitter end. No doubt, he therefore came to overestimate the importance of all that 'papal law' in the actual experience of the courts. But he never said anything to justify the view that his 'absolutely binding law' left no room for interpretation and manipulation.[44] To the charge that he too readily overlooked practices that seemed not to have heard of Rome he could reply that he had expressly allowed for that to happen. 'It is probable,' he wrote, 'that in the inferior courts . . . a law was administered that might in some sort be called customary since its main rule was the rule of thumb.'[45] To him the crucial point was whether the law that was used in those courts could be made independently from Rome: did the Church of England make its own law while holding that of Rome in high regard? Nothing that Donahue says seems to me to disprove Maitland's categorical denial of such a possibility or intention. What Donahue has shown is that the practice of those courts, though governed by the Roman canon law, was shot through with short-term devices called for by the real circumstances of disputes. This would seem to constitute the sort of further enquiry that Maitland called for. Donahue has also shown that in the actual lives of the people the canon law of distant Rome loomed much less largely than Maitland may be thought to have supposed. This is a useful correction.[46]

Thus after close on a century it looks as though Maitland's conclusions stand. The framework for discussion which he constructed still holds up, and further work on the medieval ecclesiastical jurisdiction in England still needs to be guided by it. More particularly, the Reformation was not that hiccup in continuity that Canon MacColl and even Bishop Stubbs, not to mention their modern successors, would like it to have been; for the English Church it was a revolutionary moment. Some may at times have thought that with it there came liberation; as Maitland knew very well, it was the moment when the Church exchanged one master for another. It is, of course, perfectly correct to add that its law continued mainly in the shape that centuries of direction from Rome had given it,[47] though it was a new thing for the ecclesiastical judges to pay heed to statutes made in the king's Parliament and to edicts delivered by the secular supreme head who had supplanted the pope.

What Maitland's book on the canon law demonstrated with exceptional clarity was that quite apart from his splendid gifts as a historian he had the one necessary gift without which the rest go begging. He had that good luck that springs from perfect instincts. An analysis based on so relatively limited a body of source material and so plainly underpinned by the historian's personal preferences ought to have been a great deal more vulnerable than it turned out to be.

The Common Law in Danger

In 1901 Maitland delivered the Rede lecture in the Senate House at Cambridge; before the year was out it appeared in print, enlarged by a body of notes about three times as long as the text.[48] *English Law and the Renaissance* was one of Maitland's most brilliant pieces, beautifully organized, full of

pregnant allusions, scintillating with a wit that hid its artifice
in the seeming effortlessness of composition. It must have been
great fun to listen to, and in the first instance it convinced
everybody. But some twenty-five years later it received very
critical treatment from Sir William Holdsworth,[49] and before
long it became the one of Maitland's works which everybody
agreed ran along altogether wrong tracks. Maitland, it came to
be held, had here stepped out of his territory by discussing
post-medieval developments; his own apprehension that he
had been rash 'to plunge into the sixteenth century' seemed to
be only too justified.[50] The reason for Maitland's rashness lay
in the occasion: the lecture had been founded by Sir Robert
Rede, one of Henry VIII's judges. It might hardly seem worth
going over the ground again if there had not been a recent
effort to reverse the general verdict.[51] Furthermore, the lecture
throws beams of light on Maitland's methods and attitudes,
light which has not before this been analysed. Also this is the
first time in the present book that we enter upon a piece of
ground where I can claim some experience and knowledge, so
that the temptation to discuss the Tudor century and its
treatment of the common law cannot be resisted.

Maitland's argument looks simple on the face of it. He
maintained that the early sixteenth century witnessed
throughout Europe a great revival of the Roman law – a major
effort, inspired by humanism, to get back behind the medieval
incrustations upon that law to the original source in
Justinian's codification. Everywhere men of the new learning
were lamenting the state of their country's laws and
advocating the adoption of the law of Rome; everywhere there
threatened what the Germans had come to call 'the Reception'
(of the Roman law, that is), though only in Germany did this
Reception properly take place with, it was held, the law of
ancient Rome replacing the traditional customs of the various
territories. But it could easily have happened also in England.
here too the old law had grown antiquated and evoked
frequent loud protests: it was called barbarous, incomprehensible, far too expensive, and unjust. Here too civilians (men

80

learned in the law of Rome) made themselves heard. Maitland singled out Reginald Pole, cousin and opponent of Henry VIII and in the reign of Mary Tudor the cardinal who brought England back into the papal Church, on the strength of remarks attributed to him in the treatise by Thomas Starkey which a modern editor had entitled *The Dialogue between Pole and Lupset*. Even more especially he pointed to Sir Thomas Smith, Regius professor of civil law at Cambridge and later secretary of state to Queen Elizabeth, who in his inaugural lecture drew attention to the virtues of the Roman law and the chances of employment it offered to its graduates. Maitland stressed the appearance of new courts – Star Chamber and Requests, as well as the fully grown Chancery – in all of which, so he thought, the procedure and the law used owed more to Rome than to England. He noted the great decline in the business before the common-law courts; and he pointed out that Henry VIII, who he believed wished to rule as a despot, would manifestly have found the civil law with its emphasis on the prince as sole law-giver more to his taste than the common law. Did not this king, who terminated the study of the canon law at the universities, provide new fields of activity to the civilians, in a statute which not only permitted them to practise in the Church courts but also contains 'the strongest statement of King Henry's divinely instituted headship of the church'?[52] Above all, he drew attention to the cessation of the Year Books in 1535, a cessation which he regarded as a species of death-knell for the living practice of the common law; nor would he regard the initiation of personal collections of 'Reports' by this or that lawyer as a sufficient replacement of those annual productions.

So Maitland elaborated the danger: 'In the second quarter of the sixteenth century the continuity of English law was severely threatened,' and 'in the middle of the sixteenth century and of the Tudor age the life of our ancient law was by no means lusty.' But that state of affairs did not endure, and by the early seventeenth century we find ourselves in the company of Sir Edward Coke, celebrating the virtues of a legal edifice which in his opinion had stood unaltered and unalterable from time immemorial. The common law had fought off the attacker. Thus Maitland wished to know what had enabled it to do so when other ancient laws collapsed before the Roman onslaught. In one of his neatest remarks he rejected the sentimentalities which turn up too frequently in songs of praise for the common law: 'National character, the genius of a people, is a wonder-working spirit which stands at the beck and call of every historian.' Instead he found his answer in the system which had been built around that law. Served by a regular profession, taught in established schools (the Inns of Court), the common law was far too well developed and entrenched to suffer defeat at the hands of an alien invader. 'Law schools make tough law':[53] here lay the secret of the common law's success in surviving the Renaissance.

He backed his argument with a marvellous display of learning; his notes testify to wide reading in at least four languages and, as usual with Maitland, also to acquaintance with unprinted materials. He must particularly have rejoiced when he found a saying of the sixteenth-century French jurist François Baudouin, to the effect that students of the law will find the resolution of their difficulties in the study of history, while historians 'would do better to study the development of laws and institutions than devote themselves to the investigation of armies, the description of camps of war, the tale of battles and the counting of dead bodies'.[54] Moreover, the thesis of the lecture satisfied two different groups of the devout: those who believed that Tudor government aimed at despotism, and those who celebrated the triumph of the common law. No wonder, therefore, that the printed text quickly became a piece of the universal gospel according to F.W.M.

As I have said, Holdsworth, tracking the continuity of the English common law through sixteen volumes, decided to dissent. His forty-odd pages contain much laborious and careful argument, but they can be boiled down to his refutation of the four propositions he extracted from

Maitland's lecture. In each case even more arguments could be produced than he knew. In the first place, there was the alleged decline of the law courts' business which he argued rested on mere comment; he tried to show by counting plea rolls that it had not occurred. His statistics are crude, and he was wrong; especially in King's Bench business dropped off very markedly in the years 1480–1550.[55] What neither he nor Dr Blatcher, the later historian of that court, allowed for was the notable development of the commission of oyer and terminer which transferred much of the missing business to a common-law device controlled by that court. Maitland had used a remark of the chronicler John Stow according to which the judges had in the Michaelmas term of 1557 looked around at empty courts; Holdsworth doubted the truth of the story, but since the year in question witnessed a devastating concatenation of epidemics in which, some think, twenty per cent of the nation may have died, the scene may well have happened, for reasons that say nothing about the fortunes of the courts.

Next Holdsworth reviewed the alleged attacks on the old law and justifiably identified them as a commonplace exchange of grievances which in no sense could be said to have undermined the command of the common law over the affairs of the subject. He could have added that the remarks attributed to Pole in fact expressed the mind of Thomas Starkey, a cleric trained in theology and the Roman law, and that even Starkey, aware that a total replacement was not feasible, called mainly for the codification of the common law. He might also have added that Smith's advocacy of the Roman law rather noticeably did not include any prospect of employment in the king's courts for its practitioners. The various schemes of reform, of which Maitland made much, were in fact either bits of private enterprise never taken seriously by the king's government or envisaged improvements in the training of common lawyers. Looked at more closely, the supposedly vociferous assault dwindles into a few murmurs.

Thirdly Holdsworth turned to the cessation of the Year

Books and showed that we find no lessening vigour in the Inns
or the profession. On the contrary, the common lawyers
became more articulate and inventive, a point that could have
been elaborated without end. Had Holdsworth but known it,
1535 was a year of no significance in the history of the Year
Books; it marked the end of the run that later got printed, but
manuscript Year Books survive for almost every year down to
1602.[56] Lastly, Holdsworth dealt with the alleged threat
posed by equity and by the new courts. He showed himself
aware of the central facts: equity remained a supplement to the
common law and not a rival; it owed far more to the common
law than to any other system; in the new courts the law
administered was greatly affected by the fact that common
lawyers ran those courts. He concluded that even if Henry VIII
had wanted to introduce the law of Rome he could not have
done so: the omnipresence of common lawyers in his own
administrative machine and in Parliament would have prevented him. This is essentially true, and in fact I know of no
evidence that Henry or his ministers ever remotely contem-
plated any such transfer. Maitland far too readily threw every
bit of hostility to the common law into a basket held in the
king's hand, ascribing to him purposes and initiatives which at
most belonged to private persons with little or no influence on
the rulers of the realm. On the contrary, from the 1530s
onwards common lawyers and their ultimate instrument, the
act of Parliament, successfully tightened their hold on England; before very long they even absorbed the king's divinely
ordained headship of the Church into their parliamentary
monarchy.

Thus things stood – with the Maitland thesis dead and
occasional further nails hammered into its corpse – until a few
years ago Dafydd Jenkins decided that Maitland had been very
ill-treated. It is quite true that some typically subtle reservations in the notes are neglected under the influence of the
confident text. For instance, Maitland's argument concerning
the cessation of the Year Books depends heavily on those
books being 'official' publications, a view which his note

admits may not be certain.[57] But Jenkins's 'rehabilitation' will cause misjudgments unless it is properly examined, which is a compelling reason for attending to it here, even if relatively briefly. Too much of his history has not caught up with the state of research, though he does score a few valid points of law.

Jenkins's extensive argument about the alleged hostility and quarrels between the courts of law and equity quite ignores the by now well-established understanding that what was at issue was rivalry for business, not disputes over the fundamentals of the law.[58] Whatever may have been at issue between Coke and Lord Chancellor Ellesmere, and what was at issue included a lot of personal animosity arising from matrimonial affairs, their gladiatorial performances came much too late, in the reign of James I, to affect the Maitland thesis. Jenkins has surprisingly not caught up with the discovery that the Year Books did not cease in 1535. Though Holdsworth sixty years ago did indeed concede that the supremacy, though not the existence, of the common law 'was in very serious danger', massive work done since has shown how unnecessary the concession was. I know of no evidence in statutes, plea rolls, reports or treatises that would support such a conclusion. What Jenkins says about the new courts reminds one of long-dead attacks on them that saw them as alien elements; we did not take long to discover that they were firmly in the hands of common lawyers. Moreover, they always themselves admitted the supremacy of the common law by reserving in their decrees any rights at law that the parties might be able to prove. Maitland's dubbing of the 1539 Act of Proclamations Henry's *lex regia* was one of his more unfortunate *bon mots* because it fixed the notion of an intended despotism in historians' minds, and Jenkins's attempt to rescue Maitland is both too subtle and inaccurate. The *lex regia* was the instrument by which the people of Rome transferred their own power to their emperors; it formed the, usually notional, basis of absolute imperial power. Commentators who saw here only a concession which left the source of power (as Jenkins claims) vested in the people as donors may have convinced themselves that this reservation had any meaning: one may doubt whether Tiberius or Diocletian would have agreed. In any case, Maitland was using the term allusively, believing as he did, with many others before and after him, that that act of 1539 vested absolute legislative power in the king alone, to the detriment and possible elimination of Parliament. That is what made it for Maitland the keystone of Henry's planned despotism. This misjudgment had a long history, and it would be unfortunate if Jenkins were to succeed in reviving it. The act neither could nor was meant to serve any such purpose.[59]

Thus much of Jenkins's argument stands on very shaky historical ground. However, what is really at issue is his assertion that Maitland posed a question and gave an answer to which all the criticism since Holdsworth is irrelevant. The question was, why did the common law survive in the age of the Reception, and the answer was found in its innate strength. But Maitland was mistaken in supposing that the common law was in any danger at all: his question did not exist. Jenkins calls J. H. Baker to witness who is said to have described the Rede lecture as 'completely vindicated'. What Baker regards as vindicated is Maitland's answer which, even as it turns out to be true, totally destroys the question.[60] The Reception and the dangers associated with it have turned out to be a myth which has had to be abandoned even in Germany. As Baker emphasizes, both Maitland and his critics erred in supposing that the choice lay between simple continuity and a revolution threatened by the humanist revival of Roman law. In actual fact, as he demonstrates at very convincing length, the common law in the first half of the sixteenth century underwent a transformation from within which amounted to just about as much of a revolution as replacement by the law civil might have been, though the revolution was disguised behind a façade of sameness. It was so disguised because the renewal of the common law was the work of the common law itself – work carried out by the courts and sometimes accepted or further promoted by that law's ultimate weapon, the act of

Parliament. We had occasion to note this earlier: Maitland missed this age of transformation altogether because he had committed himself to a view according to which the common law, hogtied by its antiquated 'forms of action' became ossified; like everybody else he could expect a renewal to come only from external elements – equitable and other remedies derived from the civil law, remedies which in the end were acclimatized in the continuity of the law. In actual fact, continuity was seriously interrupted by the self-renewing power of the common law.

Thus *English Law and the Renaissance*, whether one considers its main thesis or its ranging implications for the Tudor century, strayed into a cul-de-sac created by the historian's preconceptions. Once again, of course, one major cause of error was simply the state of research. Maitland's very wide reading for his lecture included none of the true evidence for what was going on in the law of England because that evidence had not yet been recognized, let alone opened up. More surprisingly it also did not include Christopher St German's *Doctor and Student*, the most distinguished legal treatise of the early sixteenth century.[61] The modern edition appeared long after Maitland's day, but the Cambridge University Library possessed the original printing. Since his day a great deal of material, some of it printed but most of it at best calendared, has been investigated, with the result that Henrician hostility to the common law and the threatening advance of the civil law have both disappeared into the lumber-room. Seventy-five years of work produce their advances, and it is, of course, no blame to Maitland that he could not anticipate them. But in other parts of his labours such inescapable defects did not, as we have seen, undermine the main theses he put forward; in respect of *English Law and the Renaissance* they did. This happened because Maitland for once, quite probably because he was venturing into a period in which lack of familiarity hampered his instinct, accepted rather than questioned the dogmas of his day. He accepted the Reception, he accepted the assurance that Henry VIII wished to be a tyrant, he accepted (as his title shows) the portmanteau use of the term Renaissance. In all these respects the doctrines of his day were simply wrong, which is why the Rede lecture, brilliant and evocative and indeed stimulating though it is, remains as the one segment of Maitland's work that is also wrong.

Maitland's Only Narrative

Some time late in 1896, Lord Acton, Regius professor of modern history at Cambridge, invited Maitland to contribute a chapter on 'The Anglican Settlement and the Scottish Reformation' to the second volume of the cooperative *Cambridge Modern History* he was beginning to plan. Acton did a good many odd things in his life, but in its small way this was as odd as any. Though Maitland had proved his quality as a historian, it was as the historian of medieval law and as one who had never produced a connected narrative. As we have seen, he himself thought himself devoid of that particular skill and, as he showed later over the *Life* of Leslie Stephen, did not relish the thought of moving into any territory where whole packs of reviewers might lie in wait for him.[62] It is possible that Acton, who wished his history to be totally impartial, a legitimate but impossible ambition for which he has since received much ridicule, wanted to commit a theme likely to flare up in controversy to one who had never been a Catholic and had ceased to be a Protestant. Maitland took some persuading. In February 1897 he put the proposal off until he had written his Ford lectures, but then he accepted. In February 1898 he was hard at work, and a year later he told Sidgwick of the promise which Acton's well-known blandishments had extracted from him. He had begun to realize that he was bound to get involved in the contemporary turmoil over the legitimacy of the Church established in 1559 – the problem of Anglican orders – and the so-called 'crisis in the church' – the disputes between high ritualists and low traditionalists.[63]

However, before he left England that winter he put the chapter into the editor's hands, with some misgivings but also much relief. 'It will be a very strange book,' he wrote, 'that History of ours. I am extremely curious to see whether Acton will be able to maintain a decent amount of harmony among the chapters. Some chapters that I saw did not look much like parts of one and the same book.'[64] I can understand his feelings: when I edited the same volume for the *New Cambridge Modern History* I had to decide that diversity would serve better than any attempt to impose uniformity.

As things turned out, it was Maitland's chapter that stuck out, sore-thumb fashion, in the book and perhaps in the whole series.[65] In the first place, it is brilliantly written – full of life, rushing along, very funny in places. Maitland left no doubt that he knew the people he was talking about; he understood their problems and their minds. An enormous amount of information is packed into it without ever destroying the verve of the story-telling, and that (as too many other chapters proved) constitutes very uncommon art. Even to this day Maitland's account of the years 1558–63 remains not only highly readable but very useful; no one else has ever constructed the European setting of those events in England and Scotland with such revealing power. The sketches of personalities, from the heights (Elizabeth, Cecil, Knox, various popes) to the lesser lights (especially the gaggle of feuding Scots lords), carry instant conviction. There are many unforgettable phrases. 'A king shall be kidnapped, and a king shall be murdered, as of old: it is the custom of the country.' 'It must probably be allowed that most of the young men of brains and energy who grew to manhood under Mary were lapsing from Catholicism, and that the educated women were falling faster and further' (a double insight too often forgotten in present assessments). 'The Lorrainers were not France: their enemies told them that they were not French.'[66] Anybody will pick his own gems, and it has been pointed out that historians going over the same ground always run the risk of unconsciously committing plagiarism.[67] Above all, there is the splendid manner in which the whole complex story remains before the reader even as its details are unravelled in successive paragraphs. Nothing relevant is skipped or evaded; we are not only told what happened but we fully understand how it came about. On the evidence of this chapter, Maitland had it in him to write exceptionally impressive narrative – to tell a tale in which the problems resolved by analysis weave in and out of the story without ever breaking it up.

This enthusiastic verdict, fully justified, has been pronounced by all who have commented on Maitland's Elizabethan phase. Some critical qualification of one's admiration is therefore not out of place. The writing is perhaps a bit too much the same throughout; even as one laps up the driving sequence of short sentences one begins to hope for the occasional respite of a longer structure, with dependent clauses, to permit a rest for reflection. The density of the material, so brilliantly marshalled in the first two thirds of the chapter, becomes tiring as the pace of events slackens and the reader's interest flags a little in the last third. Maitland's resort to pregnant allusions – they abound throughout – can deteriorate, as has been felt before, into real obscurity. When the Spanish ambassador thinks Elizabeth influenced by 'the heretic Italian friars' Maitland (rightly) guesses that he has 'Vermigli and Ochino' in mind. So far just good enough, but when we are then told that 'her eyes filled with tears over Peter Martyr's congratulations' and that 'she talked predestination with Fra Bernardino' we are expected to know that the same two people, in the same order, are meant.[68] This overdoes it: the manner becomes mannered and the style precious. There are quite a few passages which must bewilder any but the initiate. Maitland gets away with this sort of thing only because he makes the reader impatient to rush along with him. Allusiveness becomes touching when the medievalist in Maitland gets the upper hand. The state of Scottish politics calls up memories: 'When we see these things we think of the dark age: of Charles the Simple and Rolf the Pirate.' Oh yes? 'Their doings send back our thoughts to far-off Carolingian days, when the "benefice" became the hereditary fief.' They do? 'That heretics are not to rule was no new principle; the Counts of Toulouse had felt its edge in the old Albigensian days.' One can just about cope with that one.[69]

Nevertheless, a few blemishes apart, Maitland's skill as a teller of tales remains pretty marvellous. What of the contents? The secret of Maitland's success here lies in his understanding of mutual influences that hold the two parts of his theme together, and the stroke of genius appears in the device which starts the chapter with the Scottish scene before Elizabeth is brought to the throne and her dilemmas in the settlement of religion are put before us. It is this that makes the further interweaving of the countries' futures possible and thus utterly convincing. The story as Maitland told it has stood up remarkably well: he got it right not only in detail but in his distribution of emphases. His work has even survived what at one time seemed a major revision. Maitland believed that the religious settlement of 1559 reflected essentially the political and religious intentions of the queen and Cecil. Then in 1951 the late Sir John Neale put forward an ingenious new interpretation. He thought that the queen had not wanted anything as Protestant as the outcome was; she had been forced to move much further towards the Reformation by a pressure group of extremer men in the House of Commons. If that was so, much of the story needed rewriting, and it was accordingly rewritten, by Neale and others. But now we know that Neale was inventing. His pressure group never existed; his treatment of the Protestant divines as instigators of extreme measures contradicted their recorded words and sentiments; and his neglect of the Lords, where the only real opposition to Elizabeth's programme made itself felt among Catholics, totally distorted his account. Maitland had after all got it right, and in essentials we are today back with his story.[70]

Revision has been rather more successfully active in the history of the Scottish Reformation.[71] That did not come as quite so sudden a thunderclap as Maitland seemed to think; it had a longer prehistory and its full development took much longer than Maitland, following John Knox on his preaching campaign, suggests. Nor was it quite so much a mere product of noble faction politics; the movement was really carried by a group of lairds – gentry, not nobility – who in the first instance managed the preachers. Maitland unquestionably exaggerated the backwardness of Scotland in the sixteenth century: those memories of Charles the Simple and Rolf the Pirate would have been better suppressed. A closer look reveals quite a few of those characteristic Maitland touches – those words of reserve and hints at qualification. Neither the 'Scottish Renaissance' nor the early moves of reform in that country are forgotten, though it is surprising that an author who remembered David Lindsay and Alexander Alesius should have forgotten William Dunbar. As for the effect of the revolution of 1560, Maitland knew that bishops were not immediately abolished, that presbyterianism took its time to come, and that the possessions of the Scottish Church were by no means immediately secularized – though this last point is wrapped in one of his over-allusive statements.[72] All things considered, Maitland did remarkably well in extracting a reasonable narrative from the confusion he found. The Anglican Settlement had been pretty thoroughly discussed before; here his problem lay in tracing his way through the biased expositions put out by warring parties among the historians. The history of Scotland stood where it was to remain for decades after Maitland's day – in its infancy; the story of the Reformation there when Maitland wrote still amounted to nothing more than a diligent copying of John Knox's own, immensely influential account. Maitland showed he knew better.

It has to be said that if Acton chose Maitland as a man uncommitted to either side in the Reformation he may have been troubled by what he received: the chapter leaves no doubt that his author thought better of the Protestants than the Catholics. Partly he did so because he once again allowed a touch of 'whiggery' to affect him: he regarded the events in Scotland as so important because 'the fate of the Protestant Reformation was being decided and the creed of unborn millions in undiscovered lands was being determined.'[73] True enough, but a thought dangerous to the impartiality of the historian; and Maitland promptly underlined the danger by a snide, though just, remark about the sort of things people were still debating about Mary Stuart. But in part the delicately coloured bias of his narrative reflected a historical truth. England could not go back beyond the revolution of Henry VIII's reign; Elizabeth made the only possible choice when she avowed her reformed faith; the Protestants did have the right of it.

Not that this saved Maitland from the attentions of some of his contemporary Protestants. That Canon MacColl whom later he was to convict of ignorance of the canon law crossed his path while the chapter was being written. In October 1899 MacColl published an essay to prove that the Settlement of 1559 had been formally endorsed by the English Church in a meeting of its Convocation. He needed this meeting because he thought that the failure of the Marian bishops to vote for the Settlement in the House of Lords deprived the Acts of Supremacy and Uniformity of legal force: one of the estates of the realm had not consented. So, out of a misunderstood and misapplied document, he constructed himself a Church assembly which he claimed had added that consent. Maitland's answer, published three months later, must be reckoned one of the finest pieces of courteous destruction ever composed by a historian; barely hiding just contempt, it yet inflicts no wounds that could fester. 'Canon MacColl's New Convocation'[74] is a miniature masterpiece, and the overwhelming temptation to quote from it cannot be altogether resisted. 'He will agree with me,' said Maitland gravely, 'that the Roman Church has not permanently profited by a consecration that was perpetrated at the sign of the Nag's Head. He will agree with me that the Anglican Church will not permanently profit by a Convocation that is holden at the sign of the Cock and

Bull.' MacColl had found ten of the twenty-six sees vacant, nine bishops voting against the Settlement, one absent through illness and seven 'for no assignable reason'. Maitland: 'Now the Canon's memory seems to me as faulty as the equation $9 + 1 + 7 = 16 \ldots$ Is not imprisonment an assignable reason?' MacColl perpetrates a wild muddle of misstatements: 'The author of these sentences must forgive a pedagogue for saying that, had they been written in the hurry of an examination, they would have been regarded as signs of ingenuity – but of indolence also. Coming, as I hope they come, from a comfortable study, I can only wonder at them.' And so on – but temptation must now be really overcome.

However, MacColl did cause Maitland to make one concession more than was necessary. The canon had claimed as 'unquestionable' that in the sixteenth century the spiritual peers were regarded as 'the first estate of the realm' whose failure to consent would render a statute either doubtful or more probably invalid. Maitland quickly showed that the sixteenth century held no such view: bishops voted, or failed to vote, as members of the Upper House whose consent as a House was required. This surely was doctrine even before the sixteenth century, but Maitland then conceded that it may not have been universally accepted by 1559. He repeated the caution in the *Cambridge Modern History*: 'it was by no means so plain as it now is that an act against which the spiritual Lords had voted in a body may still be an act of the three Estates.'[75] He permitted himself these quite mistaken doubts partly because (as we saw before) he thought that the concept of estates had some real meaning in the history of the English Parliament, in which he was mistaken; partly because he noticed some ambassadorial comment that seemed to support MacColl (in that century ambassadors' reports on the English Parliament very rarely got anything right); and partly because he was troubled by a mysterious gap in the Lords Journal which left the crucial days undocumented. Had the pages been torn out because they might reveal the adverse vote which might be thought to invalidate an act passed by both Houses and assented to by the queen? The answer is that those pages had dropped out on the occasion of some rebinding; no sinister purpose was at work. They still existed in the early seventeenth century when a learned antiquary made a copy of the Journal in which they survive.[76] There were no reasons for Maitland's reservations, but MacColl's ghost can rest content in the knowledge that he caused his formidable adversary to insert the one error in legal history to be found in that chapter in the *Cambridge Modern History*.

Maitland's surprising but satisfactorily successful engagement with the sixteenth century resulted in by-products worth a brief word. As always he had worked very hard in the sources; though by policy not permitted footnotes, he could have justified every fact or statement in his account by references to letters available in print, in abstracts or in manuscript. But as always he had gone further, and the results appeared in five notes he called 'Elizabethan Gleanings'.[77] They were working notes for the chapter and all of them testify to his outstanding handling of historical sources mishandled or ignored before his day. The truly important one is the last, on the two famous acts of the 1559 Parliament – Supremacy and Uniformity. As he said, 'it may be rash to suppose that about these two famous statutes . . . anything remains to be said.' They had been printed and reprinted several times before, and everybody concerned had read them with care. It took a Maitland to point out that 'whatever else an act of parliament may be, it is a piece of parchment. It is preserved in the palace at Westminster. It can be inspected by the public.' So he went to look, as he always did, and found that the parchment did indeed 'tell tales' about the fortunes of both bills in their passage through Lords and Commons.[78] Much has since been made of such material, for as Maitland said the Original Acts handled in Parliament sit there in what is now the Record Office of the House of Lords, and no work on Parliament (from 1497 onwards) which has not involved studying them is worth consideration. To me, this unerring pinpointing of the crucial task of research, so fruitful in the outcome, much more even than the rogue chapter he contributed to the *Cambridge Modern History*, spells out Maitland's genius.

4 Patron Saint

The reasons for the mourning of 1906 and for the continued devotion to Maitland's memory may now have become clear. Here was a historian of exceptional energy, diligence and excellence who wrote about recondite but very important themes with clarity, wit and life, in a manner never matched before or after him – incidentally in any language known to me. Everything he said counted, to the point where even now he remains in charge of whole areas of medieval studies. Though it has proved possible, and indeed necessary, to correct Maitland here and there, the main part of his work remains alive and no question arises of interring or even embalming him. If he came back today he would find the world very strange but the world of learning quite familiar because it was he who shaped its future. Time and again we have found him standing at the start of the developments which have dominated English historical writing since his day and since he led the way. He proclaimed the need for unprejudiced and undogmatic history, and though even he can be seen occasionally as influenced by unconscious assumptions he nearly always practised precisely what he preached. He opened the road to the archives from which the history of this country has been written ever since. He himself seems to have believed that he was only returning to the principles which had guided the historians of the seventeenth and early eighteenth centuries, and he spoke with high respect of Thomas Madox.[1] Madox's works, especially the history of the Exchequer from 1066 to 1327 which he published in 1711, are indeed monuments of learning; they are also virtually unreadable and do not bear comparison with Maitland's writings or the use to which he put his knowledge of the archives. There is a universal quality about Maitland: he wished to know and understand the people of all ranks in medieval England and therefore wrote history that cannot be confined in such artificial categories as legal, or constitutional, or indeed social. It was very proper of him to acknowledge ancestry and predecessors, but today we can see that it was really he who marked the beginning of new things.

Even this, however, does not fully explain his place in the historical pantheon; in order to understand that we have to turn away from his writings and comprehend the ordinary circumstances of his life. Unlike other scholars of his day or before him, he was quintessentially a university professor, as scholars have been ever since. Unlike even Stubbs, who held a chair for exactly the same length of time as Maitland did (eighteen years) but belonged to the prehistorical, pre-Maitland, generation, he spent much of his life in the labours of teaching, examining, sitting on committees: he is one of us. Unlike just about every English university teacher at the time, and many since, he knew himself to be a member of a world-wide community, a complex that since his day has become both manifest and commonplace. Maitland travelled very little. After he grew to manhood he never visited the continent of Europe and except for his enforced winter journeys seems never to have left England. An invitation to Harvard in 1898 had regretfully to be turned down on grounds of health.[2] And yet he knew historians in Germany and Austria and the United States in ways that at the time no one else did, whereas nowadays such a multiplicity of contacts has become the norm of a scholar's life. His correspondence with people like Joseph Redlich of Vienna, George Burton Adams of Yale, John Chipman Gray and Charles Gross and James Bradley Thayer of Harvard, Melville Madison Bigelow of Boston University – all highly respected names who outlived Maitland but preceded him into oblivion – places him at the centre of an established network of scholarly intercourse. If he could not travel they came to call on him, at Cambridge or at Horsepools. Why, even Jan Smuts appears among his correspondents, newly graduated at Cambridge and anxious for a testimonial which Maitland, explaining that he had never supplied one 'with a better will', forwarded to him.[3] Maitland added a complimentary copy of *Bracton's Note-Book*. Not all of Maitland's actions set the tone of subsequent behaviour: how many professors have ever presented a three-volume work to a student who had impressed them in his examination papers? Interestingly enough, France does not seem to have entered Maitland's circle of operations – in which thing too he proved not untypical, for though later English medievalists rushed there for inspiration, French scholars to this day display only a very occasional interest in this country.

In his teaching, too, Maitland strikes a recognizable chord. As a reader and professor he never had the interesting but extraordinarily time-consuming experience of supervising undergraduates in their Colleges: he lectured, and very influentially too. It is his recognition of his purpose in teaching that here concerns us because it identifies yet another of Maitland's founding-father acts. As he explained,[4] history in his time was still a new thing in the universities and still malleable in its structure and contents; he hoped it would display 'not only the vigour but also the adaptability of youth'. He would be surprised to find how youthfully flexible, to the point of plain chaos, it has remained as it grew older. Maitland knew that others in the little volume he was introducing would dilate upon the reasons why it should be taught; for himself, he characteristically wished it to be remembered 'that, whether we like it or not, history will be written'. It will be written by all sorts of people, not only by the well known or eminent:

> Many a man is writing the history of his county, his parish, his college, his regiment, is endeavouring to tell the tale of some religious doctrine, some form of art and literature, some economic relationship, or some rule of law. Or, again, he is writing a life, or he is editing letters. Nor must we forget the journalists and the history, good, bad, and indifferent, that finds a place in their articles; nor the

reviewers of historical books, who assume to judge and therefore ought to know.

All this, he said, was 'important work' and should therefore be done right – 'well, conscientiously, circumspectly, methodically'. Those four adverbs deserve pondering: they sum up what Maitland, in thought and in practice, regarded as the criteria for history properly taught and studied. It was as well that he did not add 'with inspiration', for that ingredient, though he regularly added it himself, he could not expect to infuse into others.

The important point was 'that mankind should believe what is true, and disbelieve what is false'. Yes indeed: any historian who cannot grasp this is betraying his trust. But things had barely started in England. 'To make Gibbons or Macaulays may be impossible' – nor, I would add, specially desirable. 'But it cannot be beyond the power of able teachers to set in the right path many of those who, say what we will, are going to write history well or are going to write it ill.' Where many a colleague tried to justify the teaching of history in the universities on the grounds of public policy – on the grounds, that is, that men in public life would do their work better if they knew history – Maitland avoided this doubtful though popular claim to recognition. For him the university study of history mattered because it provided a very necessary training for historians who must be helped to do their duty well. For the last hundred years all sorts of people have been able to learn from Maitland how to do it well, even if their performances did not often reach the standard he set for himself and seemed to achieve so effortlessly. Of course, in the first place medieval historians have found him a teacher to follow, but by no means they only and not only those who had been made to meet him in their undergraduate days. A few years ago a social historian who had trained as an anthropologist and never heard of Maitland came across him almost by accident. There he found the guidance he needed to break out of the traditional opinions concerning the 'peasantry' of England and to fight his way to an interpretation so shocking to convention that the conventional have ganged up to drown him.[5] But Mr Macfarlane is unquestionably more right than wrong on the essential parts of his thesis, and it was Maitland who helped him there.

This latest disciple stands in a long line of equally grateful pupils. One could easily put together an anthology of footnotes acknowledging grateful debts to Maitland. It would be large, impressive and also rather boring, and Maitland would mock it. But it would document his influence in the way that historians should substantiate their conclusions. It is as well that Maitland's posthumous influence should have been so powerful and pervasive; he who had so much to teach could in life point to few who sat at his feet to learn how to write history. He lectured to students of law rather than history, for there were few of the latter, and those were the days, in England at least, before the arrival of the research student. Cambridge did not institute the Ph.D. degree until 1920, and even then it remained for many years a preserve for scientists. In regard to the production of young scholars Maitland once again pointed a way when he hoped to use the editing of Year Books for their training – 'an opening which might lead in course of time to a "competence", a little good repute and possibly a professorship'.[6] However, around 1900 very few people would have thought this a sensible way to prepare for a career. Maitland had one distinguished pupil (in an informal sense) in Mary Bateson, a truly promising medievalist whose early death in November 1906, three weeks before his own, distressed him deeply.[7] Not one of us but will envy her for learning her trade from Maitland living; we have to learn it from a Maitland who in ordinary terms has been dead for close on eighty years.

The climate of the day in any case hardly assisted Maitland. He might have said of himself what he said of Acton: 'A great deal of his best work here was done among grey-headed people – classical scholars and such, prone to regard history as an elegant form of trifling.'[8] The *English Historical Review* started appearing in 1886, and while it owed most to its first editors – Mandell Creighton and Reginald Lane Poole – it quickly took advantage also of the existence of a Maitland in this country. Historians, never a very clubbable lot, lacked – as in a manner they still do, and as I think they are well advised to continue doing – an organization representing them as a profession, a point which Maitland noted.[9] The Royal Historical Society had indeed been founded in 1868 but it was decades before it got out of the hands of amateurs, some well-meaning but some very distinctly not so; the first truly professional president, George Prothero, took office in 1901.[10] Here, too, Maitland set an example when he gave life, purpose and endurance to the Selden Society, an offspring of which any scholar can be proud, and an offspring also who has never ceased to celebrate the memory of its father. Founding organizations which carry on the work which one man and one life-time cannot possibly discharge is one of the best services that a man can do to the cause of learning: another lesson that Maitland taught.

It is really astonishing to realize in how many ways Maitland stood at the beginning of a journey down the right road: teacher, research scholar, writer of history based on sound methods of work, founder of societies, inspirer of others. I think it no exaggeration to say that Maitland set the standards by which we – today's working historians – live, or at least try to live, or at least ought to try to live. These are standards that are not only right but also formidable, which is what makes them worth aspiring unto. If few of us can ever hope to approach to a fulfilment of Maitland's demands on us, far fewer still can hope to do so with his instinctive touch and his grace of execution. But then we do not aspire to be Maitlands; it is enough if we can suppose that he would have thought quite well of the way in which we practise his commandments.

The historians of England have been fortunate. When at last they turned serious and professional and committed about their enterprises they had Maitland to show them the way. Other branches of learning, some of which also settled down to professional labours and university-based existence around the turn of the century – I am thinking of some social sciences, of the formal study of literature, and of bibliography – have still not fully got over the fact that their founders were often suspect in their scholarship, wayward in their standards, ungenerous and bigoted in their attitudes to others. We historians descend from a man of outstanding scholarship, unfailing standards and impeccable manners. The other side of the coin is the absence of any excuse we might have for not doing right. If Maitland, who had no one to teach him, could bequeath to us so comprehensive a lesson on our duty, what evasion shall we cultivate when we fail to do it – when we allow dogma to direct our labours or submerge real people in abstract entities? When we fail to read the sources? But the flesh, as we all know, has a habit of being weak: which is why, even today, we shall do well to keep Maitland amongst us.

Notes

ABBREVIATIONS

Maitland's works

Cam: *Select Historical Essays of F. W. Maitland*, ed. Helen M. Cam (1957)
CP: *Collected Papers*, ed. H. A. L. Fisher (3 vols; 1911)
DBB: *Domesday Book and Beyond* (1897)
ELR: *English Law and the Renaissance* (1901)
HEL: (with F. Pollock) *The History of English Law before the Time of Edward I* (2 vols; 1895; 2nd edn 1898. The 1st edn is here cited)
Letters: The Letters of Frederic William Maitland, ed. C. H. S. Fifoot (1965; cited by page references)
MP: *Memoranda de Parliamento* (1893; for the full title see ch. 3, n. 1)
RCL: *Roman Canon Law in the Church of England* (1898)

Others

Bell: H. E. Bell, *Maitland: a Critical Examination and Assessment* (1965)
SS: Selden Society

CHAPTER 1: THE MAN

1. *Cambridge University Reporter* 37 (1906–7), 526.
2. In the *New Statesman* for 4 June 1965.
3. *Cambridge University Reporter* 37 (1906–7), 1302 ff.
4. *Law Quarterly Review* 23 (1907), 137–50.
5. Cambridge University Library, Add. MS 8130, nos 2 and 20.

6. A. L. Smith, *Frederic William Maitland* (1908), 6–7, 13–17.

7. H. A. L. Fisher, *Frederick [sic] William Maitland, Downing Professor of the Laws of England: a Biographical Sketch* (1910), 177.

8. See the book by Cameron (below, n. 10), 190–4.

9. W. W. Buckland, 'F. W. Maitland', *Cambridge Law Journal* 1 (1921–3), 279–301.

10. H. E. Bell, *Maitland: a Critical Examination and Assessment* (1965); James R. Cameron, *F. W. Maitland and the History of English Law* (1961).

11. S. F. C. Milsom, 'F. W. Maitland', *Proceedings of the British Academy* 66 (1982 for 1980), 265–81.

12. C. H. S. Fifoot (ed.), *The Letters of F. W. Maitland* (1965), to be supplemented by E. L. G. Stones (ed.), *F. W. Maitland: Letters to George Neilson* (1976), and D. J. Guth and M. H. Hoeflich (eds), 'F. W. Maitland and Roman Law: an Uncollected Letter, with comments and notes,' *University of Illinois Law Review* 2 (1982), 441–8.

13. C. H. S. Fifoot, *Frederic William Maitland* (1971). This book is excellent on the facts; I hope I may be allowed to express my general indebtedness here without specific references along the way.

14. Ermengard Maitland, *F. W. Maitland: A Child's-Eye View* (1957); H. A. Hollond, *Frederick William Maitland, 1850–1906* (Selden Lecture, 1953).

15. G. R. Elton, *The Practice of History* (1967), 14.

16. G. M. Young, *Daylights and Champagne* (2nd edn, 1948), 271 ff.

17. J. P. Kenyon in the *Times Literary Supplement* of 2 March 1984, p. 222.

18. This may not be absolutely true. Maitland's letters to Leslie Stephen survive only in Fisher's memoir, where they are printed without address and subscription.

19. The two hands are illustrated in *Letters*, between pp. 280 and 281.

20. The best bibliography of writings by and about Maitland is that appended to the book by Cameron (n. 10 above).

21. Below, pp. 27–8.

22. *Letters*, 272.

23. E.g. *CP* I, 162–201; III, 304–402.

24. Below, pp. 34–6.
25. *Letters*, 372.
26. Ibid., 208, 210, 302.
27. Ibid., 212.
28. Ibid., 203–4
29. Ibid., 208, 212, 222.
30. Ibid., 213.
31. Ibid., 128.
32. *CP* I, 11.

CHAPTER 2: THE HISTORIAN

1. Burckhardt's great work on the Italian Renaissance appeared in an English translation in 1890, but in any case Maitland read German fluently and frequently.
2. Cf. his obituary notice of Stubbs (*CP* III, 495–511).
3. *CP* I, 480–97, delivered on 13 October 1888, within a week of taking up his chair.
4. Ibid., 482.
5. Ibid., 484.
6. *CP* II, 1.
7. *CP* I, 493.
8. Below, pp. 50–1.
9. Cf. my analysis in *The Sources of History: England 1200–1640* (1969).
10. *CP* I, 485–6.
11. Cf. my restrained remarks on this subject in *Studies in Tudor and Stuart Politics and Government* III, 289–304. They caused offence among the offenders, especially the Marxist interpreters of English social history.
12. *CP* I, 304–28; II, 61–80.
13. *Letters*, 195.
14. Cf. the article by Guth and Hoeflich (ch. 1, n. 12).
15. Ed. Stones (ch. 1, n. 12), *passim*.
16. *Letters*, 18–21.
17. F. W. Maitland (ed.), *Year Books 1 & 2 Edward II: 1307–9* (SS, 1903).
18. For a fuller discussion of Year Books see Elton, *1200–1640*, 174–81, and for what can be done with this material see E. W.

Ives, *The Common Lawyers of Pre-Reformation England: Thomas Kebell: A case-study* (1983).

19. Milsom, *Proc. Brit. Academy* (1982), 274.
20. *Letters*, 84–7. The letter was manifestly intended to keep Pollock away from contributing any more disastrous chapters to this allegedly joint enterprise.
21. *CP* II, 417–96, published in 1893.
22. See also his tribute to Stubbs (above, n. 2).
23. See Ermengard Maitland's memoir of her father (ch. 1, n. 14).
24. *HEL* I, 165–9.
25. *Letters*, 328.
26. *CP* I, 490–1.
27. As I have pointed out elsewhere (*Historical Journal* 27 [1984], 734–5), Herbert Butterfield's famous 'whig interpretation of history' was really lawyers' interpretation; the essence of the method, oddly enough, infiltrated also Marxist historiography by way of the Christian preoccupation with the future rather than the past which Marxism adopted in a secularized form.
28. The review, which appeared in *The Athenaeum* of 21 October 1899, is reprinted in Cam, 259–65.
29. *Letters*, 203, 214.
30. Ibid., 181.
31. Ibid.
32. Especially Bell's study which covers the ground to about 1960.
33. Cf. T. F. T. Plucknett, *Early English Legal Literature* (1958), 3: 'Maitland took a delight in manipulating language and was careful about mood and tense. An impersonal construction, which dissociates him from the statement which follows, may very well indicate a doubt or question which at the moment he was unable to pursue further.'
34. I am grateful to Col. Frederick Bernays Wiener for his kind help in identifying errors in Maitland's work.
35. James Tait, *The Medieval Borough* (1936), esp. pp. 26–7, 340–58.
36. *CP* II, 44.
37. Two of the three volumes projected have appeared: SS vols 72 (1955) and 89 (1971). The third, due out shortly, will contain an introduction with a full explanation of *Fleta* and its significance.
38. The work was done by another admirer of Maitland, V. H. Galbraith; see esp. *Domesday Book: Its Place in Administrative*

History (1974), ch. 1.

39. See esp. Maitland's discussion of 'The History of the Register of Original Writs', *CP* II, 110–73.

40. The best study of the Register is Elsa de Haas and G. D. H. Hall (eds), *Early Registers of Writs* (SS, vol. 87, 1970); for the effect upon Maitland's work see F. B. Wiener, 'The Register of Writs: Seed-Bed of the Common Law', *American Bar Association Journal* (1971), 498–504.

41. The crucial work was done by R. van Caenegem in his edition of *Royal Writs in England from the Conquest to Glanvil* (SS, vol. 77, 1958–9), and in his Maitland Lectures, *The Birth of the English Common Law* (1973).

42. *HEL* I, 129.

43. *CP* II, 172.

44. H. G. Richardson and G. O. Sayles (eds), *Select Cases of Procedure without Writ under Henry III* (SS, vol. 60, 1941).

45. G. O. Sayles (ed.), *Select Cases in the Court of King's Bench, vol. IV* (SS, vol. 74, 1955).

46. I am thinking of that splendidly fruitful piece of shameless fiction, the Bill of Middlesex. See Marjorie Blatcher, *The Court of King's Bench 1450–1550: a Study of Self-Help* (1978).

47. *CP* II, 172.

48. *Equity, alsc the Forms of Action at Common Law* (1910), 360 ff.

49. Below, pp. 86–7.

50. Cf. F. B. Wiener, 'Bracton – a Tangled Web of Legal Mysteries that Defied Solution for More than Seven Centuries', *George Mason University Law Review* 2 (1978), 129–65, for a full and lively rehearsal of what has happened to Bracton.

51. S. E. Thorne, *Bracton on the Laws and Customs of England* (4 vols, 1968, 1977).

52. The fullest statement of Milsom's views is found in his Maitland Lectures, *The Legal Framework of English Feudalism* (1976); see also his introduction to the 1968 reprint of *HEL* (here cited as 'Introduction'). For his attitude to Maitland and an important analysis of the fundamental differences between Maitland's and his own approach see his lecture on Maitland (ch. 1, n. 11).

53. 'Introduction', p. xxxvi.

54. Van Caenegem in his SS vol. 77, p. 315 also regrets Maitland's

invention of the misleading term for these assizes.

55. Milsom, *Legal Framework*, 181–2.
56. 'Introduction', p. xlviii.
57. *HEL* II, 1.
58. Below, pp. 64–6.
59. See *Proc. Brit. Academy* (1982), 277. Maitland himself gave superficially better grounds to Pollock (*Letters*, 86), but the manner in which he explained his position certainly hints at a determination to keep Pollock away from the enterprise.
60. *HEL* II, 1.
61. *HEL* I, pp. xxxiv–xxxv.
62. *Proc. Brit. Academy* (1982), 275.
63. Ibid., 273–5.
64. *Letters*, 65.

CHAPTER 3: FOUR CASES

1. *Records of the Parliament holden at Westminster, on the 28th Day of February, 1305* (Rolls Series, 1893). For the genesis of the edition see *Letters*, 55, 68–72, 96–8, 101–2. The central part of the introduction is reprinted in the collections made by Hazeltine and Cam; the last, as the most accessible, is used here. Maitland analysed the character and history of the roll in the first part of his Introduction, an impressive technical discussion not reprinted later.
2. A. L. Smith, cited in Cam, p. xvii.
3. *Constitutional History*, 74–6.
4. Cam, 62 n. 1, 94 n. 3.
5. Ibid., 78.
6. Ibid., 94.
7. C. H. McIlwain, *The High Court of Parliament and its Supremacy* (1910).
8. C. H. McIlwain, *Constitutionalism and the Changing World* (1939), 9.
9. A. F. Pollard, *The Evolution of Parliament* (1920). The second edition of 1926 contains some pretty brash retorts to criticisms offered by medievalists.
10. Ibid., 3.
11. Pollard had become a victim to Oxford's determination to

appropriate the Cambridge historian. The book originated in a fellowship at All Souls College conferred upon him in 1908 on condition that he pursued 'researches suggested by the late F. W. Maitland' (ibid., p. v).

12. G. O. Sayles, *The King's Parliament of England* (1975), with an excellently full bibliography.

13. G. O. Sayles, *The Medieval Foundation of England* (1948; 2nd edn 1950), 458. The role played in this development by war and the money it demanded has since been thoroughly investigated by G. L. Harriss, *King, Parliament and Public Finance in Medieval England to 1369* (1975).

14. Sayles, *King's Parliament*, 108.

15. For a sane review and balancing verdict see E. Miller, *The Origins of Parliament* (Hist. Association Pamphlet G. 44, 1960).

16. B. Wilkinson, *Studies in the Constitutional History of the Thirteenth and Fourteenth Centuries* (1937), ch. 1.

17. J. G. Edwards, '"Justice" in Early English Parliaments', *Bulletin of the Institute of Historical Research* 27 (1954), 35–53; and *The Second Century of the English Parliament* (1979).

18. For this assertion, which goes counter to some old and recent convictions, see my *Studies in Tudor and Stuart Politics and Government* (3 vols, 1974, 1983), nos 22, 34, 35.

19. Cam, 92.

20. Cited by J. G. Edwards in *Bull. Inst. Hist. Res.* 27 (1954), 40.

21. Sheila Lambert, *Bills and Acts* (1971), esp. 91-6.

22. *Letters*, 143–4, 182, 328–9.

23. *RCL*, 35, 44.

24. Ibid., 31–2.

25. Ibid., 26–30.

26. Ibid., 52–4.

27. See esp. ibid., 90–4.

28. Reactions and developments down to ca. 1960 are briefly discussed in Bell, ch. VIII.

29. *Letters*, 195.

30. *RCL*, 48.

31. Ibid., 130–1.

32. Margaret Bowker (ed.), *An Episcopal Act Book for the Diocese of Lincoln 1514–20* (Lincoln Record Soc. 61, 1967).

33. The attack was inserted into the 8th edition of MacColl's popular book on *The Reformation Settlement* (1900); for

Maitland's reply see *CP* III, 137–56.

34. A. Ogle, *The Canon Law in Medieval England* (1912): 'ill-conceived, perverse and misleading' (C. R. Cheney, *Medieval Texts and Studies*, 159 n. 2).

35. C. Duggan, *Twelfth Century Decretal Collections and their Importance in English History* (1963). In sum he argues that Maitland was mainly right, but not so much on the grounds of the evidence he cited.

36. J. W. Gray, 'Canon Law in England: some reflections on the Stubbs–Maitland controversy', *Studies in Church History* III (ed. G. Cuming, 1966), 48–68. He belongs to those medievalists who hold that the Reformation legislation only confirmed what was already fact, a position I cannot accept.

37. E. W. Kemp, *An Introduction to Canon Law in the Church of England* (1957), 20–1.

38. C. Donahue, 'Roman Canon Law in the Medieval English Church: Stubbs v. Maitland re-examined after 75 years in the light of some records from the church courts', *Michigan Law Review* 72 (1974), 647–716. He notes the criticisms listed above but seems to think that they damage Maitland.

39. Donahue, 655–6.

40. B. Woodcock, *Medieval Ecclesiastical Courts in the Diocese of Canterbury* (1952), 89–92, cited Donahue, 661; Woodcock, I think rightly, sees nothing odd in this.

41. Donahue, 665–7.

42. On this see now R. A. Houlbrooke, *Church Courts and the People during the English Reformation 1520–1570* (1979).

43. Donahue, 678.

44. Ibid., 698: he reads 'absolutely' not in Maitland's sense ('inescapably') but in a sense which it could not have had at the time – 'exclusive of all modification'.

45. *RCL*, 42–3.

46. Donahue (704) gets from Maitland the impression of an embattled English Church 'struggling to enforce every jot and tittle of the papal law in the face of ever-increasing royal pressure to limit the field of application of that law'. It is not an impression that I ever sensed in reading *RCL*, and I wonder if anyone else has. I would, however, agree, as I have already said, that Maitland overstated the consistent purposiveness of royal action.

47. See the lecture by R. H. Helmholz, *Canon Law and English Common Law* (SS, 1983), which demonstrates some interesting continuities and interactions but does not sufficiently emphasize that by his own account virtually all that mutual influence occurred after the break with Rome.

48. *English Law and the Renaissance* (1901). The text is reprinted in Cam, 135–51, but virtually all the learning enshrined in the notes is there omitted.

49. W. S. Holdsworth, *A History of English Law* IV (1924), 252–93. See also my remarks in *Studies* (above, n. 18), II, 74–5, written in 1951; we have learned a lot more about these matters since.

50. Stones (ch. 1, n. 12), 27.

51. D. Jenkins, 'English Law and the Renaissance. Eighty Years on: in Defence of Maitland', *Journal of Legal History* 2 (1981), 107–42.

52. *ELR*, 62. This, alas, is not true; the statute uses language quite commonplace since the creation of the royal supremacy in the Church in 1534.

53. Ibid., 25.

54. Ibid., 58 (my translation).

55. See Blatcher (ch. 2, n. 46), ch. II, esp. her table on p. 21.

56. Jennifer Nicholson, *Register of MSS of Year Books Extant* (Hist. MSS Commission for SS, 1956).

57. See Maitland's very reserved note, *ELR*, 77, which differs quite a bit from the impression left by his text, 21–2. Two years later Maitland no longer thought the Year Books official (above, p. 27). On the Year Books see also A. W. B. Simpson, 'Source and Function in the Later Year Books', *Law Quarterly Review* 87 (1971), 94–118.

58. W. J. Jones, *The Elizabethan Court of Chancery* (1967), esp. Part III.

59. Jenkins, 110; Maitland, *ELR*, 19, 69. The long debate about the intent of the act is reviewed and settled in R. W. Heinze, *The Proclamations of the Tudor Kings* (1975), ch. 6.

60. J. H. Baker (ed.), *The Reports of Sir John Spelman* (SS, 1977), II, 28.

61. St German gets one mention in the notes, as one of the people complained of by the northern rebels of 1536 (*ELR*, 81–2).

62. *Letters*, 86, 371.

63. Ibid., 158, 172, 195.
64. Ibid., 212.
65. 'The Anglican Settlement and the Scottish Reformation', *Cambridge Modern History* II, ch. 16; reprinted in Cam, 152–210. The reprint will be cited here.
66. Cam, 153, 167, 181.
67. Bell, 127, n. 3, convicts Conyers Read (biographer of Francis Walsingham and William Cecil) of just that. In this particular case I am driven to wondering whether the plagiarism was unconscious.
68. Cam, 167.
69. Ibid., 155, 157, 165.
70. J. E. Neale, 'The Elizabethan Acts of Supremacy and Uniformity', *English Hist. Rev.* 67 (1951), 304–32, and *Elizabeth I and her Parliaments*, I (1953), 51–84. He was followed, e.g., by G. R. Elton, *England under the Tudors* (1955), 271–4, and J. Hurstfield, *Elizabeth I and the Unity of England* (1960), 31–2. Maitland was restored by the most thorough investigation of the whole episode: N. L. Jones, *Faith by Statute: Parliament and the Settlement of Religion 1559* (1982).
71. See esp. G. Donaldson, *The Scottish Reformation* (1960), and I. B. Cowan, *The Scottish Reformation: Church and Society in Sixteenth Century Scotland* (1982).
72. Cam, 188.
73. Ibid., 152.
74. *CP* III, 247–58, reprinted in Cam, 247–58.
75. Cam, 177.
76. Eliza Jeffries Davis, 'Journal of the House of Lords for April and May 1559', *English Hist. Rev.* 28 (1913), 531–42.
77. Reprinted from ibid., 1900, in *CP* III, 157–209, and in Cam, 211–46.
78. Cam, 229–46.

CHAPTER 4: PATRON SAINT

1. *Letters*, 128.
2. Ibid., 179.
3. Ibid., 121.
4. See Maitland's introduction to *Essays on the Teaching of*

History (put together by a body of historians and published by the Cambridge University Press in 1901), pp. xvii–xix.

5. Alan Macfarlane, *The Origins of English Individualism* (1978).
6. *Letters*, 242.
7. Ibid., 388–9.
8. Ibid., 261.
9. *Teaching of History*, p. xix.
10. For the history of that remarkable body, the like of which for virtue as well as for lack of it no other country possesses, see R. A. Humphreys, *The Royal Historical Society 1868–1968* (1969).

Index

Reception, 80, 86–7
Rede, Sir Robert, 79–80
Redlich, Joseph, 3, 98
Reformation, 72, 74, 91–3
Renan, Joseph Ernest, 37
Requests, court of, 68, 81
Richard II, 28
Richardson, H. G., 40, 63
Rolf the Pirate, 91–2
Rolls Series, 27, 57
Round, John Horace, 37–8
Royal Historical Society, 102

St German, Christopher, 87
Sayles, George O., 40, 44, 63–4
Scotland, 60, 68, 88–9, 91–3
Scott, Sir Walter, 16
Seeley, Sir John, 1
Seisin, 45–7, 53
Selden Society, 9–10, 27–8
Sidgwick, Henry, 6, 8, 15, 17, 73
Smith, A. L., 3
Smith, Sir Thomas, 80, 83
Smuts, Jan, 98–9
Spelman, Sir Henry, 47
Spencer, Herbert, 19
Star Chamber, court of, 31, 42, 68, 81
Starkey, Thomas, 80, 83
Stenton, Sir Frank, 33

Stephen, Leslie, 7, 10, 105 n.18
Stow, John, 83
Stubbs, William, 20, 22, 31, 57–9, 64, 70–1, 73–4, 77, 79, 98

Thayer, John Bradley, 98
Thorne, Samuel E., 34, 43–4
Tout, Thomas Frederick, 33
Tractarians, 6, 70
Trespass, writ of, 41–2
Turner, G. J., 28

Van Caenegem, Raoul, 41, 44, 108 n.54
Vinogradoff, Paul, 7–8, 14

Walsh, William, 70
Westminster, 59, 63
Whittaker, W. J., 12
Wiener, Frederick Bernays, 107 n.34
Wilkinson, Bertie, 64
Writs, procedure by, 32, 40–2, 53; Register of, 40–2

Year Books, 13, 26–8, 32, 81, 84–5, 112 n.56
York, diocese of, 77

Zocca-Rosa, A., 3